# GROUND BEEF
# GROUND BEEF
# GROUND BEEF
# GROUND BEEF

To my family
and friends
who endured my failures
as well as my successes.

# The GROUND BEEF Cookbook

Illustrated by Mike Nelson

by
Joanne Waring Lindeman

A Nitty Gritty Book*
Published by
Nitty Gritty Productions
P.O. Box 5457
Concord, California 94524

*Nitty Gritty Books—Trademark
Owned by Nitty Gritty Productions
Concord, California

ISBM 0-911954-46-5
Library of Congress Catalog Card Number: 78-52044

# TABLE OF CONTENTS

# INTRODUCTION

Ground beef is the all-time American favorite. Good taste, low price, good nutritive value and versatility have made it so. Creative cooks in other countries have also learned to stretch meat dollars while serving attractive and satisfying meals. Native spices are used in regional recipes to transform ordinary ground beef into taste-pleasing sensations.

Many of the recipes in this book were acquired during travels in other countries. The rest have been collected over the years from friends and relatives.

Beef consumption in this country averages 95 pounds per capita per year. An estimated 40 percent of the beef consumed is ground, which adds up to 38 pounds per person per year . . . now that's a lot of hamburger!

You will encounter three varieties of ground beef in your shopping. Fat content greatly affects price of each.

**GROUND BEEF** is made from meat trimmings containing about one-third fat. It is suitable for broiled hamburgers and recipes calling for the meat to be cooked and fat drained off—as in casseroles.

**GROUND CHUCK** is ground from the chuck section and contains less fat— making it perfect for meatballs and meat loaves.

**GROUND ROUND** is the leanest of all. This variety is great for diet burgers, Steak Tartare (page 6), and Beef Burgers Wellington (page 144).

**GINDING YOUR OWN** is best. With the aid of a food processor, it takes no time at all. This enables you to control fat content, meat quality, and freshness. Watch for "specials" on chuck steaks and roasts. Trim away bones and fat and process according to the manufacturer's directions.

Freshly ground meat should be stored loosely wrapped in the refrigerator no longer than 24 hours after purchasing. To avoid spoilage, it is really best to buy ground meat the day you intend to cook it, or freeze it for later use.

Store ground beef in the freezer not more than 3 months. It should be thawed in the refrigerator to prevent bacteria growth that can occur if left too long at room temperature. Frozen meat used in recipes calling for browned beef may be cooked slowly in a skillet while it's still frozen. Also, frozen meat patties can be cooked in the frozen state. Thawed meat should never be refrozen because it is likely to be unsafe to eat.

The ingredients called for in the recipes which follow are easily found in supermarkets and specialty food stores. For best results please use the quality of ground beef that is called for, since fat content can make a difference in some recipes.

I hope this book will be helpful when you are looking at that pound of ground beef and wondering "What am I going to do with it?" Try something new and enjoy!

Joanne Lindeman

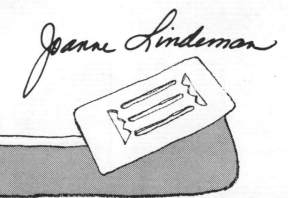

3

# APPETEASERS

# STEAK TARTARE

I use my food processor for chopping the meat, it's fantastic. Your meatman can do the same, but be sure he doesn't grind the meat in a machine previously used for pork. Serve with French, rye or pumpernickel bread.

2 lbs. freshly ground sirloin
1-1/2 tsp. salt
1 tsp. coarse ground pepper
3 tbs. oil
1 tbs. wine vinegar
1 tsp. Dijon mustard
dash of Tabasco
3 tbs. drained capers

1/4 cup minced onion
4 mashed anchovies
1 tbs. Worchestershire sauce
1 egg yolk
garnish with: whole anchovies
             sprigs of parsley
             gherkin pickles, sliced

Combine meat, salt, pepper, oil, vinegar, mustard, Tabasco, capers, onion, anchovies and Worchestershire. Mound mixture on large platter. Make a well in center to place raw egg yolk. Garnish and serve with bread. Serves 6 to 8 guests.

# BARBARA'S BEEF DIP

Serve with taco chips.

2 lbs. ground beef
1 onion, finely chopped
2 cloves garlic, minced
2 cans (8 ozs. ea.) tomato sauce
1/2 cup catsup
2 tsp. sugar
1-1/2 tsp. oregano
2/3 cup grated Parmesan cheese
2 pkg. (8 ozs. ea.) cream cheese, softened

Cook beef, onion and garlic until lightly browned and crumbly. Drain off fat. Stir in tomato sauce, catsup, sugar and oregano. Simmer slowly 10 minutes. Remove from heat. Add cheeses and stir until melted. Keep warm in chafing dish. Serve with taco chips. Leftovers may be frozen. Serves 6 to 8 guests.

# ELEGANT MUSHROOMS

Quick, easy and delicious!

1 lb. fresh mushrooms
2 tbs. butter
1/3 lb. ground round
1 tsp. salt
1/2 tsp. garlic powder
1/4 tsp. lemon pepper
2 tbs. minced onion
1/2 cup mayonnaise

Remove stems from mushrooms and save for future use. Heat butter in skillet and briefly saute mushroom caps. Combine beef, salt, garlic powder, lemon pepper and onion. Add mayonnaise to moisten. Stuff mushrooms and broil 3 mintues or until meat is bubbly. Serves 4 to 6 guests.

# STUFFED MUSHROOMS

1 lb. large fresh mushrooms
1/2 lb. ground beef
1 pkg. (8 ozs.) cream cheese, softened
1 tsp. Worchestershire sauce
1 tsp. lemon pepper
1 cup (4 ozs.) grated Jack cheese
1/4 tsp. garlic powder
1/2 tsp. onion powder
1 tbs. minced parsley
3 tbs. grated Parmesan cheese
1 tsp. crushed tarragon

Clean mushrooms. Remove stems and save for future use. Brown beef in skillet until crumbly. Drain off fat. Mix with cream cheese and remaining ingredients. Fill mushroom caps with mixture. Place on broiler pan or cookie sheet. Broil 5 inches from heat for 3 minutes. (Also delicious served without broiling!) Serves 6 to 8 guests.

9

# CRISP WON TON

Sweet-Sour Dipping Sauce, page 11
1/2 lb. ground round
1/2 lb. ground lean pork
6 raw shrimp, chopped
4 water chestnuts, finely chopped
2 tbs. chopped green onions
1/2 tsp. sugar
1 egg, beaten
2 tbs. cilantro or Chinese parsley
1 tsp. cornstarch
1 tsp. salt
1 pkg. (16 ozs.) won ton wrappers
oil for frying.

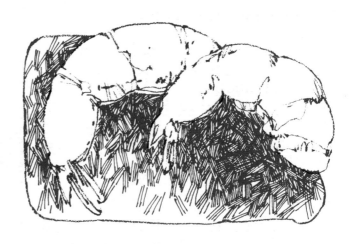

Prepare sauce and keep warm over hot water. Combine meats, shrimp, chestnuts, onions, sugar, egg, cilantro, cornstarch and salt. Place one teaspoonful of mixture in center of each won ton wrapper. Fold into triangles. Moisten sides with water and seal by pressing together with spoon or fork. Fry in hot oil 375°F. until brown. Serve with Sweet-Sour Dipping Sauce. Makes 4 dozen.

## SWEET-SOUR DIPPING SAUCE

1/2 cup sugar
1/2 cup vinegar
2 tbs. soy sauce
2 tbs. dry sherry or sake
3 tbs. catsup
2 tbs. cornstarch
1/2 cup pineapple juice

Combine sugar, vinegar, soy sauce, sherry and catsup in saucepan. Bring to boil. Mix cornstarch with pineapple juice. Blend into soy sauce mixture. Cook until thickened.

# TINY CORNISH PASTIES

1 pkg. (11 ozs.) pie crust sticks
1/2 lb. ground beef
1 small onion, minced
1 clove garlic, crushed
2 small peeled potatoes,
    finely diced

1 tsp. Spice Islands Beau Monde seasoning
1/4 tsp. pepper
1/4 cup beef bouillon
milk
1 egg white

Mix pie crust sticks according to package directions. Roll out pastry on lightly floured surface. Cut out circles with 3-inch round cookie cutter. Mix beef, onion, garlic, potatoes, Beau Monde, pepper and bouillon. Place a teaspoonful of mixture on half of each pastry circle. Fold the circles into half-moon shapes. Moisten edges with pastry brush dipped in milk and seal with fork tines. Brush tops with egg white and prick with fork. Bake on cookie sheet in 400°F. oven 25 minutes, until golden brown. Makes about 30.

# SAMOSAS

These spicy Indian turnovers may be refrigerated or frozen until ready to fry. Use won ton skins if making appetizers as you want them to be smaller.

Chutney Yogurt Sauce, page 15
1-1/2 lbs. ground beef
1 onion, minced
3 cloves garlic, crushed
2 tbs. curry powder
1 tsp. cumin
1/2 tsp. ground ginger

1-1/2 tsp. salt
1/8 tsp. cayenne
1 tsp. sugar
1 tbs. chopped fresh coriander or cilantro
1/2 pkg. (5 ozs.) frozen peas, thawed
1 pkg. (16 ozs.) won ton or egg roll skins
oil for deep frying

Prepare sauce and refrigerate until needed. Brown beef and onion in skillet until meat is crumbly. Drain off fat. Add garlic, curry powder, cumin, ginger, salt, cayenne, sugar and fresh coriander. Cook, stirring, for 3 minutes. Add peas and stir 1 minute longer. Set aside until filling is cooled. Place 1-1/2 tablespoons of filling in center of won ton or egg roll skin. Fold edges over to form a triangle. Seal edges with water. Heat 2 inches of oil until hot, about 425°F. Fry triangles, 2 or 3 at a time, until golden. Drain on paper towels. Keep warm in 200°F. oven until all are cooked (if you can keep your guests away from them). Serve with Chutney Yogurt Sauce.

CHUTNEY YOGURT SAUCE

2 cups (16 ozs.) plain yogurt
1/4 cup chutney, chopped
1 tsp. cardamom

Combine all ingredients and refrigerate 1 hour to blend flavors.

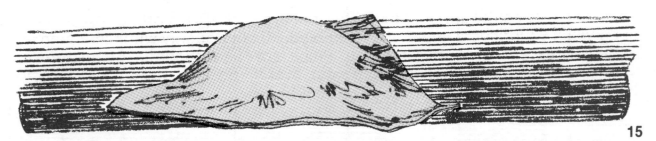

# BOW TIES

1 lb. ground beef
1/4 tsp. garlic powder
1 tsp. ground dill
1/2 tsp. dry mustard
1 tsp. salt
1/4 tsp. pepper
1 pkg. (8 ozs.) cream cheese, softened
1/2 cup finely minced green onions
1 can (8 ozs.) water chestnuts, drained and finely minced
1 pkg. (16 ozs.) won ton wrappers

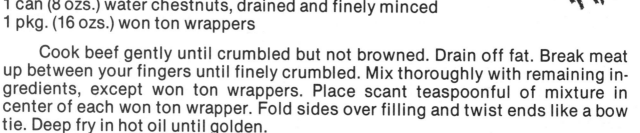

Cook beef gently until crumbled but not browned. Drain off fat. Break meat up between your fingers until finely crumbled. Mix thoroughly with remaining ingredients, except won ton wrappers. Place scant teaspoonful of mixture in center of each won ton wrapper. Fold sides over filling and twist ends like a bow tie. Deep fry in hot oil until golden.

16

# BITTERBALLEN

2 tbs. butter
1 tbs. minced onion
3 tbs. flour
1 cup milk or stock
2 tbs. minced parsley
1 tsp. salt
1 tsp. Worchestershire sauce
1/2 tsp. dry mustard

1/4 tsp. curry powder
1 lb. ground veal
2 cups (8 ozs.) shredded Gouda cheese
1 cup fine dry bread crumbs
2 eggs
2 tbs. water
oil for frying

Melt butter in medium saucepan. Saute onion until transparent. Blend in flour. Gradually add milk or stock, stirring constantly. Stir until thickened, about 8 minutes. Add parsley, salt, Worchestershire, mustard, curry powder, veal and cheese. Simmer 5 minutes. Cover and chill several hours. Dip hands in cold water and shape chilled mixture into tiny balls. (May be frozen at this point.) Roll balls in crumbs. Beat eggs with water. Dip balls in egg mixture and roll in crumbs again. Refrigerate 1 hour or overnight. Fry in hot oil (375°F.) until browned. Drain on paper towels. Makes about 80.

# COCKTAIL MEATBALLS WITH CURRY CREAM SAUCE

1 lb. ground chuck
1 lb. pork sausage
1 tsp. basil
1 can (8 ozs.) water chestnuts, finely minced
paprika
Curry Cream Sauce

Combine chuck, sausage, basil and water chestnuts. Mix well. Shape mixture into small meatballs, using a heaping teaspoonful for each. Place in baking dish. Sprinkle with paprika. Bake in 375°F. oven 15 minutes. Remove from oven. Drain off fat. Sprinkle with more paprika. Return to oven. Bake 15 minutes longer. Drain. Serve on wooden picks for dipping into sauce. Makes 8 dozen.

CURRY CREAM SAUCE —Beat together 1 package (8 ounces) softened cream cheese and 1/2 cup sour cream. Add 1-1/2 teaspoons curry powder, 1/4 teaspoon pepper, 1 tablespoon lemon juice and seasoned salt to taste. Mix well.

# DILLED MEATBALLS

1-1/2 lbs. ground beef
1 lb. ground veal
1 can (4-1/2 ozs.) deviled ham
2/3 cup milk
2 eggs
1 cup soft French bread crumbs
1 small onion, grated or minced
1 tsp. salt
1/4 tsp. ground cloves

1/4 tsp. pepper
2 tbs. butter
2 tbs. flour
1/2 tsp. Jane's Krazy Mixed-Up Salt
1 cup water
1 cup sour cream
1 tbs. catsup
1 tbs. chopped fresh dill

Combine ground meats, deviled ham, milk, eggs, bread crumbs, onion, salt, cloves and pepper. Shape into small balls. Brown a few at a time in large skillet. Drain off fat. Melt butter in small saucepan. Blend in flour and salt. Gradually add water, stirring constantly for 1 minute or until thickened. Blend in sour cream, catsup and dill weed. Heat thoroughly but do not boil. Pour sauce over meatballs and serve. Makes 10 to 12 servings.

# GUESS WHAT? MEATBALLS

Conversation will come easily at your next party with these surprises.

1-1/2 lbs. ground beef
1/2 lb. pork sausage
1 egg
1 cup dry bread crumbs
1 small onion, grated
2 tbs. Worchestershire sauce

Fillings: whole salted almonds
pineapple tidbits
green pepper pieces
salami chunks
rolled anchovy fillets
pickle cubes
stuffed or ripe olives
cheese cubes

Combine beef, sausage, egg, bread crumbs, onion and Worchestershire sauce. Shape 1 tablespoon of meat mixture around each of different fillings until all the meat is used. Heat large skillet and brown meatballs on all sides. Keep warm in chafing dish. Serve with wooden picks, and guess what? Makes about 75 meatballs.

# MANHATTAN 24-HOUR MEATBALLS

1-1/2 lbs. ground chuck
1 slice bread, crumbled
1 egg, beaten
1 tsp. salt
1 tbs. catsup
2 tbs. oil
1 small onion, minced
1 clove garlic, crushed
1/4 tsp. salt

1/4 tsp. oregano
2 tsp. flour
1 beef bouillon cube
1 cup water
1 tsp. dry mustard
2 jiggers Rye whiskey
1/2 tsp. Angostura bitters
1 jigger sweet vermouth

Combine meat, bread, egg, salt, and catsup. Shape into tiny meatballs. Heat skillet and brown meatballs on all sides. Remove meatballs. Drain off fat and heat oil in skillet. Add onions, garlic, salt and oregano. Cook until onions are tender. Blend in flour. Add remaining ingredients. Bring to a boil. Lower heat and cook until slightly thickened. Return meatballs to sauce. Simmer gently for 5 minutes. Cover and refrigerate 24 hours. Heat thoroughly before serving on wooden picks. Makes 50 meatballs.

# HAWAIIAN PUPUS

Promounced "Poo-Poohs," which means appetizers in Hawaiian.

1 lb. ground chuck
1 cup shredded coconut
1 onion, minced
2 cloves garlic, crushed
1 tsp. ground coriander
1/2 tsp. cumin
1 tsp. Accent

1 tsp. salt
1/4 tsp. pepper
1/4 cup bread crumbs
1 tsp. lemon juice
1 egg, beaten
1 can (5 ozs.) Macadamia nuts, chopped
1/4 cup oil

Combine beef, coconut, onion, garlic, coriander, cumin, Accent, salt, pepper, bread crumbs, lemon juice, egg and nuts. Shape into tiny balls. Heat oil in large skillet and fry meatballs on all sides. Drain on paper towels. Serve with wooden picks. Makes 50 meatballs.

# MEXICAN APPETIZERS

Muy Bueno!

1 lb. ground chuck
1 tbs. sugar
1/4 tsp. ground cloves
1/4 tsp. cinnamon
1 tsp. salt
1/2 cup chopped raisins
1 can (4 ozs.) diced Ortega green chiles
1 egg, beaten
1 tbs. dry sherry

Combine all ingredients. Shape into tiny balls. Arrange on ungreased, rimmed baking sheet. Bake in 500°F. oven 12 to 15 minutes, turning occasionally. Serve with wooden picks. Makes about 60 meatballs.

23

# MONGOLIAN MINIATURES

The 5 spice powder and sesame oil are essential to this recipe and should not be omitted.

1-1/2 lbs. ground chuck
1/4 tsp. Dynasty 5 spice powder
1 tsp. Worchestershire sauce
1/2 tsp. ginger
1 clove garlic, crushed
1 egg
1/4 cup soy sauce
1 tsp. sesame oil

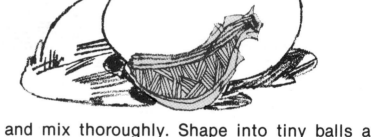

Combine all ingredients and mix thoroughly. Shape into tiny balls and brown on all sides in large skillet. Keep warm in chafing dish and serve with wooden picks. Makes about 60.

# TEMPURA BALLS

A light, crispy batter coats these unusual meatballs.

1 lb. ground chuck
1/2 tsp. salt
1 tsp. Accent
1/4 tsp. pepper
2 cloves garlic, crushed

1 tbs. soy sauce
1 cup Bisquick
1 cup cornstarch
1 cup ice water
oil for deep frying

Combine beef, salt, Accent, pepper, garlic and soy sauce. Shape into tiny balls. Heat skillet and brown meatballs on all sides. Remove meatballs from pan. Drain off fat. Mix Bisquick, cornstarch and water. Heat 1-inch of oil in large skillet to 425°F. or use deep fat fryer. Dip cooked meatballs in batter. Fry until golden. Drain on paper towels. Serve with wooden picks and Dipping Sauce. Makes 60 meatballs.

DIPPING SAUCE — Combine 1/4 cup soy sauce, 1/4 cup sake or dry sherry and 1 teaspoon sugar. Serve in an attractive bowl.

# SAVORY SOUPS AND SANDWICHES

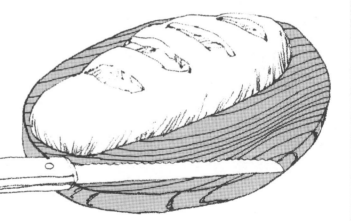

# BEEF RAMEN

Kids love it! So quick, you will too.

1 lb. ground beef
1 tsp. salt
1 bunch green onions, minced
1 cup chopped vegetables: spinach, zucchini, mushrooms,
                          lettuce, celery, peas or leftovers
3 pkgs. (3 ozs. ea.) Top Ramen Noodles

Saute beef until crumbly. Drain off fat. Add salt, onions and vegetables. Cook 2 minutes. Prepare Ramen noodles according to package directions. Add beef and vegetables. Cook until liquid evaporates, about 3 minutes. Pass the soy sauce and enjoy. Makes 4 servings.

# DANISH BEEF SOUP

1 tbs. butter
1 onion, chopped
2 cloves garlic, crushed
1-1/2 lbs. ground beef
1 can (16 ozs.) tomatoes, undrained
2 cans (10 ozs. ea.) beef consomme
2 soup cans water
2 cups diced raw potatoes

1/2 cup chopped green pepper
1/2 cup dry red wine
2 tbs. paprika
1-1/2 tsp. salt
1 tsp. pepper
1 tsp. caraway seed
1 tsp. marjoram, crumbled
Cheese Toast

Melt butter in large saucepan. Brown onions, garlic and beef until crumbly. Drain off fat. Add remaining ingredients. Stir, breaking tomatoes into small pieces. Bring to a boil. Reduce heat and simmer 20 minutes. Prepare Cheese Toast. Serve 2 slices on each bowl of soup. Makes 6 to 8 servings.

CHEESE TOAST — Spread butter on 16 small slices of sweet French bread. Place under hot broiler and lightly toast on both sides. Top each slice with shredded Danish cheese (about 1 cup total). Return to broiler until cheese melts.

# GOULASH SOUP

Nice on a cold evening when a simple but nourishing meal is desired. Serve with a salad and French bread.

1-1/2 lbs. ground chuck
1 cup chopped onion
1 cup cubed raw potatoes
1 cup sliced carrots
1/2 cup diced celery
1 cup shredded cabbage
2-1/2 cups (#2 can) tomatoes
1/4 cup raw rice

1 small bay leaf
1/2 tsp. thyme
1/4 tsp. basil
2 tsp. salt
1/8 tsp. pepper
1-1/2 cups water
1-1/2 cups (6 ozs.) grated cheddar cheese

In kettle, cook beef with onion until lightly browned. Pour off fat. Add potatoes, carrots, celery, cabbage and tomatoes. Bring to boil. Pour in rice and stir. Add bay leaf, thyme, basil, salt, pepper and water. Cover and simmer 1 hour. Serve with grated cheese. Makes 6 servings.

# MEXICAN CHILI SOUP

1 lb. ground beef
1 clove garlic, minced
1/2 bell pepper, diced
1/2 onion, chopped
1 can (11 ozs.) chili beef soup
1 can (10-3/4 ozs.) tomato soup
2 soup cans water
salt and pepper
2 tbs. minced cilantro or Chinese parsley
1 cup (4 ozs.) grated cheddar cheese

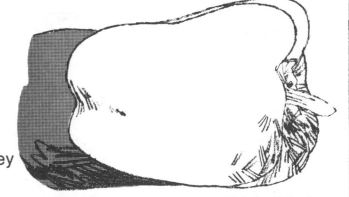

Brown beef, garlic, bell pepper and onion in skillet. Drain off fat. Stir in soups, water, salt, pepper and cilantro. Heat to serving temperature. Serve garnished with cheddar cheese. Makes 4 to 6 servings.

# SOPA DE ALBONDIGAS

1-1/2 lbs. chorizo (Mexican sausage)
1-1/2 lbs. ground round
2 cloves garlic, minced
1 tbs. minced parsley
1 tsp. salt
1/2 cup soft bread crumbs
1 egg, beaten
1 tbs. chopped fresh mint
1/4 cup oil
1 onion, minced
3 qts. beef stock
3 carrots, sliced
3 zucchini, sliced
1 can (15 ozs.) Reese baby corn-on-the-cob
fresh cilantro or Chinese parsley

Remove casing from chorizo. Mix sausage with ground round, 1 garlic clove, parsley, salt, bread crumbs, egg and mint. Shape into 1-inch balls. Heat 2 tablespoons oil in large frying pan. Brown meatballs. Remove and drain on paper towels. Heat remaining oil in large kettle. Add onion and remaining garlic. Cook until onion is transparent. Add stock, carrots and zucchini. Bring to boil. Carefully drop meatballs into boiling broth. Reduce heat, cover and simmer 30 minutes. Cool soup and skim excess fat from surface. Add drained baby corn and heat to serving temperature. Garnish with chopped cilantro. Makes 6 to 8 servings.

# ARMENIAN STUFFED PITA BREAD

1 lb. ground beef
2 tbs. oil
1 bunch green onions, chopped
1 small zucchini, finely chopped
4 tomatoes, chopped
1 red bell pepper, chopped
1 tsp. garlic salt

1 tsp. Spice Islands Mixed Herbs
2 tsp. chili powder
2 tbs. cilantro or coriander, chopped
1 cup Spanish stuffed green olives, sliced
1/2 cup salted peanuts
4 rounds pita bread

Saute beef until crumbly in large skillet. Drain off fat. Remove meat and set aside. Heat oil in skillet. Add green onions, zucchini, tomatoes and bell pepper. Saute 5 minutes. Stir in garlic salt, mixed herbs, chili powder, cilantro and tomato sauce. Add olives and peanuts. Slice pitas in half to form pockets and stuff with mixture. Makes 4 servings.

# MEXICAN TORTAS

These stuffed rolls are a real picnic pleaser. Make in the morning or the day before and store in the refrigerator. All you need is the beer, wine or soda.

1 lb. hamburger
1 can (16 ozs.) refried beans
4 French rolls
1-1/2 cups sliced cooked chicken
4 slices Jack or cheddar cheese

1 large tomato, sliced
1 large avocado, sliced
4 lettuce leaves
4 tsp. chopped green chiles
mayonnaise

Brown hamburger until crumbly. Drain off fat. Add refried beans and stir until warm. Cut tops off of rolls lengthwise. Scoop out soft centers. (Save for bread crumbs.) Spoon bean mixture into rolls then add remaining ingredeints. Replace tops and open your mouth wide. Serve at room temperature. Makes 4 servings.

# TACOS CON CARNE

1 lb. ground beef
1 bell pepper, chopped
1 onion, minced
1 tbs. chili powder
1 tsp. coriander
1/2 tsp. cumin
1 tsp. salt
1/4 tsp. pepper
1/2 tsp. sugar

1 can (8 ozs.) tomato sauce
1/2 cup chopped stuffed green olives
2 tbs. oil
1 tbs. wine vinegar
2 cups shredded lettuce
2 tomatoes, chopped
12 (4-1/2 oz. pkg.) taco shells
1 cup (4 ozs.) grated cheddar cheese

Saute beef, bell pepper and onion until beef is crumbly. Drain off fat. Stir in chili powder, coriander, cumin, salt, pepper and sugar. Add tomato sauce and olives. Simmer about 10 minutes, stirring until liquid has reduced. Heat taco shells in 325°F. oven 5 minutes. Mix oil and vinegar. Toss half of mixture with lettuce and pour remaining over tomatoes. Toss gently to mix. Spoon some of meat mixture into each shell. Top with lettuce, tomatoes and cheese. Makes 12 tacos.

# QUICK PIZZAS

1/2 lb. ground beef
1/2 lb. pork sausage meat
1 clove garlic, crushed
1 can (8 ozs.) tomato sauce
1 tsp. Spice Islands
    Italian Herb Seasoning
2 rounds pita bread
2 tbs. olive oil

1 can (2 ozs.) anchovy fillets (optional)
1/2 cup chopped bell pepper
2 green onions, minced
1 cup sliced fresh mushrooms
1 can (2-1/4 ozs.) sliced ripe olives
1/2 lb. mozzarella cheese, grated
1/2 cup grated Parmesan cheese

Brown beef and sausage in skillet. Drain off fat. Add garlic, tomato sauce and Italian herb seasoning. Simmer, uncovered, 5 minutes. Cut pita bread in half crosswise to make 4 rounds. Brush each side of cut pita with olive oil and place on cookie sheet. Spread meat sauce on each piece. Sprinkle anchovies, bell peppers, onions, mushrooms, olives and cheese evenly over top. Bake in a 475°F. oven 8 minutes or until cheese is melted. Makes 4 servings.

# FANCY PATTIES

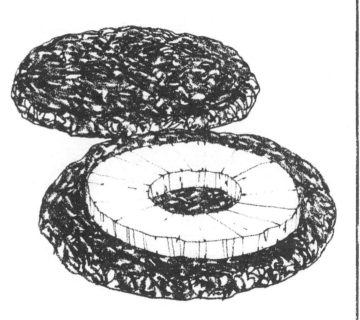

# BEEF PATTIES PARMESAN

1-1/2 lbs. ground chuck
2 tbs. minced parsley
1/4 tsp. garlic powder
1-1/2 tsp. salt
1/4 tsp. pepper
1/4 cup seasoned bread crumbs
1/4 cup grated Parmesan cheese

2 eggs
1 tbs. water
1/2 cup flour
1/4 cup vegetable oil
6 slices mozzarella cheese
1 can (15-1/2 ozs.) spaghetti sauce
Parmesan cheese

Combine beef, parsley, garlic powder, salt and pepper. Shape into 6 flat patties 1/2-inch thick. Mix bread crumbs with Parmesan. Beat eggs with water. Coat each patty with flour. Dip into egg then coat with bread crumb mixture. Allow to dry 30 minutes. Heat oil in large skillet. Brown patties on both sides. Arrange in 12 x 8 x 2-inch baking dish. Top each patty with a slice of mozzarella. Pour spaghetti sauce over all. Sprinkle with Parmesan cheese and bake in 400°F. oven 25 minutes. Makes 6 servings.

# BIFF A LA LINDSTROM

A super Swedish hamburger.

1-1/2 lbs. ground round
2 boiled potatoes, diced
2 eggs
4 tbs. light cream
2 pickled beets, finely diced
2 tbs. minced onion
2 tbs. minced capers
salt, pepper and paprika
1/2 cube (1/4 cup) butter

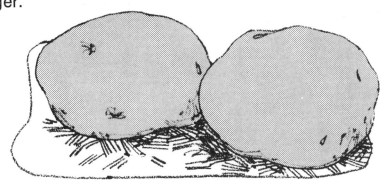

Thoroughly mix beef, potatoes, eggs, cream, beets, onion, capers, salt, pepper and paprika. Shape into 4 patties. Heat butter in skillet. Fry patties 3 or 4 minutes on each side. Makes 4 servings.

41

# BEARNAISE MUSHROOM PATTIES

Turn beef patties into elegant fare. Serve with stuffed tomatoes, fresh string beans and brown rice.

1-1/2 lbs. ground chuck
2 cloves garlic, crushed
1 egg, beaten
2 tbs. minced parsley
1 tsp. salt
1/4 tsp. pepper
1/2 lb. fresh mushrooms, chopped
Bearnaise Sauce, page 43

Combine beef, garlic, egg, parsley, salt, pepper and mushrooms. Shape into 4 patties. Broil or pan fry 4 minutes on each side. Top with Bearnaise Sauce. Makes 4 servings.

## BEARNAISE SAUCE

3 tbs. wine vinegar
1 shallot or garlic clove, minced
1 tsp. tarragon
1 tsp. chervil
dash of mace
2 egg yolks
2 tbs. cold water
1 cube (1/2 cup) butter

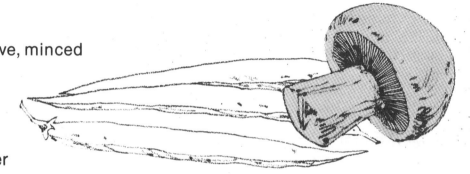

    In small saucepan combine vinegar, shallot, tarragon, chervil and mace. Cook uncovered until vinegar has reduced to 1 tablespoon. Remove from heat and set aside. Beat egg yolks with water. Melt butter. Gradually add butter to egg yolks, beating constantly. Beat egg mixture into vinegar and herbs. Heat over very low heat, stirring until thickened.

# BOMBAY BURGERS

2 tbs. butter
3 tbs. chopped green onion
1-1/2 lbs. ground round
1/2 cup mayonnaise
1 egg
3 tbs. prepared mustard
1 tbs. horseradish

1 tsp. salt
1/2 tsp. curry powder
1/2 tsp. cumin
1/2 cup peanuts
Worchestershire sauce
2 hard-cooked eggs, thinly sliced

Melt butter in frying pan. Saute onion until tender. Combine with ground round, mayonnaise, egg, mustard, horseradish, salt, curry, cumin and peanuts. Form into 6 patties. Broil, or grill over hot coals. Cook about 5 minutes on each side. Sprinkle each patty with Worchestershire before turning. Remove to warm platter. Garnish with egg slices. Makes 6 servings.

# CARPETBAG BURGERS

Marinated cucumbers and tomatoes go well with these oyster stuffed burgers.

1-1/2 lbs. ground sirloin
1 tsp. lemon pepper
1 tsp. Jane's Krazy Mixed-Up Salt
1/2 pint small shucked oysters
juice of 1 lemon
1 tbs. chopped parsley
1/4 cup melted butter
salt and pepper to taste

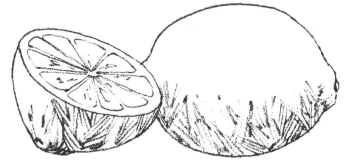

Combine beef, lemon pepper and salt. Shape into 6 patties. Place oysters on top of 3 patties. Cover with remaining patties, pressing edges to enclose oysters. Sprinkle with lemon juice and barbeque over hot coals 8 minutes on each side. Combine parsley, melted butter, salt and pepper. Pour over burgers and serve. Makes 2 to 3 servings.

# DANISH BEEFSTEAK WITH ONIONS

Boiled new potatoes and beets are a great accompaniment for this dish.

3 or 4 onions, sliced
1-1/2 cubes butter or margarine
3 tbs. water
2 lbs. ground round
1/2 cup flour
1/2 tsp. paprika

1/4 tsp. allspice
1 tsp. salt
1/4 tsp. pepper
8 eggs
1 can (10-1/2 ozs.) condensed beef broth

In large skillet fry onions in 1/2 cube butter 20 minutes or until brown. Add water and continue cooking until water has evaporated. Remove onions and keep hot. Shape beef into 8 patties. Mix flour with paprika, allspice, salt and pepper. Coat patties with seasoned flour. Melt remaining cube of butter in skillet. Brown patties 3 or 4 minutes on each side. Remove and keep hot. Fry 8 eggs. Top each patty with onions and fried egg. Blend 3 tablespoons of remaining seasoned flour with pan drippings. Gradually add beef broth. Bring to a boil and stir until thickened. Serve with beefsteaks. Makes 8 servings.

# DIJON BURGERS

Really elegant hamburgers!

1 clove garlic, minced
1 lb. ground chuck
1/4 cup dry vermouth
1-1/2 tbs. Dijon-style mustard
1/8 tsp. thyme
1/4 cup butter
1/4 cup whipping cream
watercress for garnish

   Mix garlic with meat. Shape into 4 patties. Blend vermouth, mustard and thyme in small saucepan. Heat to simmering. Set aside. Broil burgers 4 inches from heat. Allow 4 to 5 minutes for each side. Return wine mixture to high heat. Add butter and cream. Boil until sauce is thick and golden, stirring constantly. Pour over burgers. Garnish with watercress. Makes 4 servings.

# HAWAIIAN HAMBURGERS

My son Michael's favorite recipe.

1-1/2 lbs. ground beef
1 can (8-1/4 ozs.) pineapple slices, drained
2 tbs. hosin sauce (available where oriental foods are sold)
2 tbs. soy sauce

Divide meat and form into 8 patties. Flatten patties until 1/2-inch larger than pineapple slices. Place 1 slice of pineapple on each of four patties. Cover pineapple with remaining patties. Press edges together, enclosing pineapple. Mix hosin sauce with soy sauce. Brush each side of patties with mixture. Broil or barbeque over hot coals, 4 minutes each side. Makes 4 servings.

# KOREAN BURGERS

1 lb. ground beef
2 green onions, minced
1 clove garlic, minced
1-1/2 tbs. soy sauce
1 egg
2 tsp. brown sugar
1/2 tsp. Accent
1 tsp. minced fresh ginger
1 tsp. sesame seed, toasted
1 tsp. sesame oil

Combine ingredients and form into 4 patties. Broil or barbeque over hot coals 3 to 5 minutes each side. Makes 4 servings.

# PEANUT BURGERS

2 lbs. ground beef
2 eggs, slightly beaten
1/2 cup chunk-style peanut butter
1 small onion, minced
1/2 tsp. garlic powder
1 tsp. salt
1/2 tsp. Schilling Seasoned Pepper
dill pickle slices
8 hamburger buns

   Combine beef, eggs, peanut butter, onion, garlic powder, salt and pepper. Shape into 8 patties. Broil or cook over hot coals 4 to 5 minutes each side. Top with pickle slices and serve on buns. Makes 8 servings.

# PIZZA BURGERS

1-1/2 lbs. ground chuck
1/2 cup tomato sauce
1/4 cup chopped fresh mushrooms
6 anchovy fillets, minced
2 cloves garlic, minced
1/4 tsp. pepper
6 thin slices mozzarella cheese

Place beef, tomato sauce, mushrooms, anchovies, garlic and pepper in bowl. Mix thoroughly, but gently. Shape into 6 patties. Broil, pan broil or grill over hot coals. Cook 5 minutes on first side. Turn. Top with cheese slices. Continue cooking until desired doneness and cheese is melted. Makes 6 servings.

# TERIYAKI BURGERS

A simple treat that goes well with asparagus or your favorite green vegetable.

1 lb. ground beef
3 tbs. soy sauce
3 tbs. sake or dry sherry wine
2 cloves garlic, minced
1 tsp. sugar
1/2 tsp. ground ginger

Combine all ingredients and shape into 4 patties. Barbeque 4 or 5 minutes on each side. Serve on toasted sesame hamburger buns. Makes 4 servings.

# TOKYO BURGERS

Hosin sauce is available in oriental food stores. It will keep in the refrigerator for months if stored in a covered container. It is also excellent for basting barbequed chicken or spareribs.

1 lb. ground beef
2 tbs. hosin sauce
1 tbs. soy sauce
1/4 tsp. garlic powder
1/2 tsp. Accent
1/2 tsp. ground or fresh ginger
1 can (4 ozs.) sliced mushrooms, drained
2 tbs. minced green onion
4 sesame seed buns, toasted

Combine beef, hosin sauce, soy sauce, garlic powder, Accent, ginger, mushrooms and green onions. Shape into 4 patties. Pan fry or barbeque over hot coals for 3 minutes each side. Serve on sesame seed buns. Makes 4 servings.

# WORLDLY MEATBALLS

# ARMENIAN MEATBALLS

Serve on wooden picks for an appetizer or over rice for a delicious entree.

Yogurt Sauce, page 57
1 cup soft bread crumbs
1/4 cup water
1 egg
1/2 lb. ground chuck
1/2 lb. ground lamb
1/4 cup minced onion
1 tsp. salt

1/4 tsp. thyme
1/4 tsp. cinnamon
1/4 tsp. allspice
1/4 tsp. pepper
2 tsp. lemon juice
1/4 cup finely chopped almonds
2 tbs. butter

Prepare sauce and set aside. In a large bowl combine bread crumbs, water and egg. Let stand 5 minutes. Add beef, lamb, onion, salt, thyme, cinnamon, allspice, pepper, lemon juice and almonds. Shape mixture into 1-inch balls. Melt butter in large skillet. Brown meatballs on all sides. Remove from pan and drain on paper towels. Add to sauce and heat. Serve in chafing dish for appetizer or over rice as an entree. Makes about 60 meatballs or 6 entree servings.

## YOGURT SAUCE

1 tbs. butter
2 tbs. flour
1 cup Campbell's chicken broth
1 cup (1/2 pt.) plain yogurt
1/2 tsp. salt
1/4 tsp. thyme
1 tbs. minced parsley
1 tsp. lemon juice

Melt butter in medium saucepan. Blend in flour. Gradually add chicken broth. Stir until sauce thickens, about 7 minutes. Add yogurt, salt, thyme, parsley and lemon juice. Heat slowly. Makes about 2 cups.

# CARAWAY MEATBALLS WITH POTATO DUMPLINGS

In Germany these are called Kummel Klops

1 lb. ground beef
1 tsp. salt
1/4 tsp. poultry seasoning
1/4 tsp. pepper
1/4 cup bread crumbs
1/4 cup milk
1 tbs. minced parsley

1 egg, slightly beaten
1 can (10-1/2 ozs.) condensed beef broth
1 can (3 ozs.) chopped mushrooms, drained
1/2 cup minced onion
1 cup sour cream
1 tbs. flour
1 tsp. caraway seed

Combine beef, salt, poultry seasoning, pepper, bread crumbs, milk, parsley and egg. Shape into 1-inch balls. Heat large skillet and brown meatballs on all sides. Drain off fat. Add beef broth, mushrooms and onion. Cover and simmer 20 minutes. Mix sour cream with flour and caraway seed. Stir into meatballs. Cook gently for 5 minutes. Serve with Potato Dumplings. Makes 4 to 6 servings.

## POTATO DUMPLINGS

2 lbs. potatoes
2 eggs, slightly beaten
1 cup flour
1/2 cup farina (cream of wheat)
1 tsp. salt
minced parsley

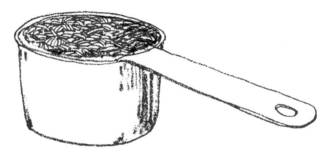

Peel and quarter potatoes. Boil until tender. Put through ricer or mash completely. Let cool. Add eggs, flour, farina and salt. Beat well. Shape into golf-sized balls. Drop into boiling, salted water. Simmer 20 minutes. Lift dumplings out and sprinkle with minced parsley. Serve immediately.

# DOUBLE BEEF AND BARLEY STEW

1-1/2 lbs. chuck steak
flour
2 tbs. oil
1 onion, chopped
2 cloves garlic, crushed
1 lb. ground chuck
1 tsp. Spice Islands Beau Monde seasoning

1/2 tsp. sesame seed
1 can (14 ozs.) beef broth
1/4 cup pearl barley
2 cups sliced carrots
1/2 cup chopped celery
1/2 cup water
salt and pepper to taste

Trim fat and bones from steak. Cut meat into bite-sized cubes. Dust with flour. Heat oil in Dutch oven and brown meat on all sides. Remove from skillet and set aside. Add onion and garlic to pan. Cook until onion is transparent. Push to sides of pan. Combine ground chuck, Beau Monde and sesame seed. Shape into small balls and brown on all sides. Return steak cubes to pan. Add broth and barley. Cover and simmer 45 minutes. Add carrots, celery and water. Cover and simmer 30 minutes or until meat is tender. Salt and pepper to taste. Makes 4 to 6 servings.

# EASY MEATBALL STROGANOFF

Serve over cooked egg noodles or steamed rice.

2 lbs. ground chuck
2 eggs, beaten
1 can (10-3/4 ozs.) cream of mushroom soup
1 pkg. (1-3/8 ozs.) onion soup mix
1/2 cup water
1/2 cup dry white wine
1 cup (1/2 pint) sour cream
parsley for garnish

Mix beef and eggs together. Shape into small balls. Brown slowly on all sides. Drain off fat. In large bowl, combine soup, soup mix, water and wine. Pour over meatballs. Cover and simmer 15 minutes. Blend in sour cream just before serving. Garnish with chopped parsley. Makes 6 servings.

# FRENCH MEATBALLS

If you love French onion soup, you'll love this.

1-1/2 lbs. ground round
1/2 cup French bread crumbs
1/2 cup cream
1 egg
1 small onion, grated
3 cloves garlic, crushed
2 tbs. minced parsley
1 tsp. salt

1/2 tsp. pepper
1 pkg. (1-3/8 ozs.) dry onion soup mix
1 qt. boiling water
3 tbs. flour
3 tbs. water
1 loaf sour dough French bread
1-1/2 cups grated Gruyere or Jack cheese
parsley for garnish

Combine beef, bread crumbs, cream, egg, onions, garlic, parsley, salt and pepper. Shape into small balls. Combine soup mix and boiling water in large pot. Carefully drop meatballs into boiling soup. Reduce heat and simmer 20 minutes. Remove meatballs to heated platter. Mix flour with water and stir into soup. Cover and simmer 5 minutes. Return meatballs to sauce. Slice bread into 1-inch thick slices and toast under broiler. Place in bottom of 9 X 12-inch baking dish.

Pour meatballs and sauce over bread slices. Sprinkle evenly with cheese. Broil 6 inches from broiler until cheese is bubbly and golden. Sprinkle with parsley. Makes 6 to 8 servings.

# FRIKADILLER

1 can (2 ozs.) anchovy fillets
1 lb. ground chuck
1/2 lb. *each* ground veal and pork
4 slices bread, crumbled
1/2 cup milk
3 eggs
1 small onion, minced
2 tbs. grated lemon rind
1 tsp. Spice Islands Beau Monde seasoning

1/2 tsp. pepper
2 beef bouillon cubes
1 qt. water
1/4 cup butter
1/4 cup flour
1/2 tsp. sugar
1/2 cup dry white wine
2 tbs. drained capers
1 tbs. lemon juice

Drain and mince anchovies. Combine half of anchovies with next 10 ingredients. Shape into small balls. In large saucepan combine bouillon cubes and water. Bring to boil and carefully add meatballs. Reduce heat and simmer, uncovered, 15 minutes, or until thoroughly cooked. Melt butter in another saucepan. Blend in flour and sugar. Gradually add wine and 2 cups of meatball broth. Stir constantly until thickened. Add capers, lemon juice and remaining anchovies. Serve sauce over meatballs. Sprinkle with parsley. Makes 8 servings.

# GREEK MEATBALLS AVOGOLEMONO

Serve with rice and steamed artichokes—yummy!

1/2 lb. ground round
1/2 lb. ground lamb
1/2 cup chopped onion
1/3 cup rice
1/3 cup milk
1 egg slightly beaten
1 tsp. salt

1/4 tsp. pepper
1/2 cup minced parsley
1 beef bouillon cube
2 cups boiling water
2-1/2 tbs. lemon juice
2 eggs, beaten

Thoroughly combine beef, lamb, onion, rice, milk, egg, salt and pepper. Form into 1-inch balls. Roll in minced parsley. Dissolve bouillon cube in boiling water. Add meatballs. Cover and simmer gently (DO NOT BOIL) for 30 minutes. Remove meatballs and keep warm. Beat lemon juice with eggs. Stir a small amount of hot liquid into egg mixture. Return egg mixture to hot bouillon. Cook, stirring, until mixture thickens. Serve lemon sauce over meatballs. Makes 4 to 6 servings.

# HOBO DINNERS

1 lb. ground beef
4 medium potatoes, cut in small chunks
4 carrots, cut in 1/2 inch pieces
2 onions, coarsley chopped
1 cube (1/4 lb.) butter
1 pkg. (1-3/8 ozs.) dry onion or mushroom soup mix

Shape meat into small balls. Place equal amounts of meatballs and vegetables on 4 large squares of heavy-duty aluminum foil. Dot each serving generously with butter. Sprinkle with soup mix. Seal foil tightly. Cook on barbeque grill 45 minutes or bake in 350°F. oven one hour. Makes 4 servings.

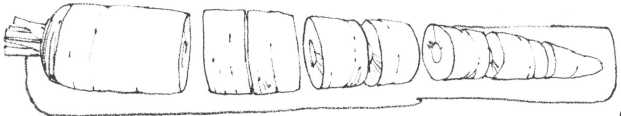

# ITALIAN SKILLET DINNER

A favorite combination that is quick and easy to prepare.

1 lb. mild Italian sausages
1 lb. ground beef
2 tsp. Kitchen Bouquet
2 cans (1 lb. ea.) stewed tomatoes
1 tsp. Italian seasoning
2 cans (1 lb. ea.) whole potatoes, drained

1 pkg. (10 ozs.) frozen Italian
green beans
3 tbs. flour
3 tbs. water
salt and pepper
Parmesan cheese

Slice sausages one inch thick. Brown in electric frying pan or large skillet. Mix ground beef with Kitchen Bouquet and shape into small meatballs. Push sausage to one side of pan and brown meatballs. Drain off all fat. Add tomatoes, Italian seasoning, potatoes, and green beans. Cover and simmer 10 minutes. Blend flour with water and stir into stew. Cover and cook 10 minutes longer or until beans are tender. Add salt and pepper to taste. Garnish with grated Parmesan. Makes 4 to 6 servings.

# KOREAN MEATBALLS

Tofu or bean curd is used often in oriental cookery. It is very high in protein and available in supermarkets and where oriental foods are sold.

1 pkg. (12 ozs.) bean sprouts
1 lb. ground chuck
1 block (16 ozs.) tofu (bean curd)
1/2 cup soy sauce
2 tbs. sugar
1 cup finely chopped green onions
3 cloves garlic, mashed

1/4 cup sesame seed, toasted and ground
1 egg
1 cup dry bread crumbs
1/4 tsp. Accent
2 tbs. sesame oil
sesame oil for frying

Parboil bean sprouts 3 minutes. Drain and rinse in cold water. Chop into 1/2-inch lengths. Squeeze out excess water. Combine with meat in large mixing bowl. Place tofu in a piece of cheesecloth. Squeeze to remove water. Mash tofu and add to meat. Mix soy sauce and sugar together. Add to meat along with the next 7 ingredients. Mix well. Shape into small balls. Heat a small amount of sesame oil in skillet. Brown meatballs on all sides. Makes 6 to 8 servings.

69

# KOFTA KARI

3/4 lb. ground chuck
3/4 lb. ground lamb
1/4 tsp. cayenne pepper
1 small onion, minced
1 clove garlic, minced
1-1/2 tsp. salt
2 tbs. chopped cilantro
1/4 tsp. nutmeg
2 tsp. curry powder
1/4 cup plain yogurt
1 egg, beaten
1 qt. beef stock
1 bay leaf
2 cloves garlic, minced
1-1/2 tsp. tumeric

1/2 tsp. salt
1/4 tsp. cumin
1/2 tsp. ginger
2 tbs. lemon juice
1/2 cup raisins
1/4 cup chopped bell pepper
1 unpeeled apple, chopped
3 tbs. cornstarch
1/2 cup half and half
6 cups steamed rice
condiments: shredded coconut, chutney
chopped green onions
peanuts, sliced bananas
chopped hard-cooked eggs
crumbled cooked bacon

Combine beef, lamb, cayenne, onion, garlic, salt, cilantro, nutmeg, curry powder, yogurt and egg. Mix thoroughly. Shape into small balls. Brown meatballs on all sides in large skillet. Drain off fat. Remove meatballs to large saucepan. Add stock, bay leaf, garlic, tumeric, salt, cumin, ginger, lemon juice, raisins and bell pepper. Simmer, uncovered, 10 minutes. Add apple. Cover and simmer 10 minutes longer. Combine cornstarch with half and half. Stir into sauce and cook until thickened. Serve with rice and condiments. Makes 6 servings.

# MEATBALLS IN MARSALA SAUCE

2 tbs. olive oil
1 onion, chopped
1 clove garlic, minced
1 tsp. salt
1/4 tsp. pepper
1/2 tsp. basil
1/2 tsp. oregano

1 cup Marsala wine
1 can (16 ozs.) tomatoes
1 can (6 ozs.) tomato paste
1-1/2 cups water
Meatballs, page 73
1 lb. spaghetti, cooked
Parmesan cheese

Heat olive oil in large saucepan. Brown onion and garlic. Add salt, pepper, basil, oregano and 1/2 cup Marsala. Cook until wine evaporates. Add tomatoes, tomato paste and water. Cover and simmer gently 1-1/2 hours, stirring occasionally. Prepare meatballs while sauce is simmering. Add remaining 1/2 cup Marsala and meatballs to sauce. Cook uncovered 10 minutes longer. Serve over spaghetti. Sprinkle with Parmesan cheese. Makes 4 servings.

## MEATBALLS

1 lb. ground chuck
1/2 cup milk
1/2 cup seasoned bread crumbs
1 small onion, finely minced
2 tbs. chopped parsley
2 tbs. grated Parmesan cheese
1 egg, beaten
1 tsp. salt
1/4 tsp. pepper
1 tsp. oil

    Combine beef, milk, bread crumbs, onion, parsley, Parmesan, egg, salt and pepper. Form into balls. Heat oil in skillet. Brown meatballs on all sides. Drain on paper towels and add to sauce.

73

# NORWEGIAN MEATBALLS

2 tbs. butter
1 small onion, minced
1 lb. ground beef
1/4 lb. ground pork
1/2 cup milk
1/2 cup fresh bread crumbs
1 egg, beaten
1 tsp. salt

1/4 tsp. pepper
2 tsp. sugar
1/4 tsp. allspice
1/4 tsp. nutmeg
3 tbs. flour
1 cup water
1 cup heavy cream
salt and pepper to taste

Heat butter in skillet and saute onion until golden. Combine beef, pork, milk, bread crumbs, egg, salt, pepper, sugar, allspice, nutmeg and sauteed onion. Shape into tiny balls. Heat skillet and brown meatballs on all sides. Remove meatballs and set aside. Drain off all but 3 tablespoons of fat. Stir flour into pan drippings. Gradually add water and cream and stir until thickened. Season with salt and pepper. Return meatballs to sauce and gently heat through. Makes 4 to 6 servings.

# PERSIAN MEATBALLS

1 lb. ground beef
1/2 lb. ground lamb
1/4 cup chopped parsley
1 cup minced celery
1/2 cup raw rice
1/4 cup water
1/2 cup bulgar
1/2 tsp. basil

1/2 tsp. chopped cilantro
2 eggs, beaten
8 hard-cooked eggs, shelled
3 beef bouillon cubes, crumbled
1-1/2 quarts boiling water
1/4 cup tomato sauce
1/2 tsp. paprika
2 tbs. chopped parsley

Combine meats, parsley, celery, rice, water, bulgar, basil, cilantro and beaten eggs. Divide mixture into 8 portions. Shape each portion around a hard-cooked egg. Place in large kettle. Dissolve bouillon cubes in boiling water and pour into kettle. Add tomato sauce and sprinkle with paprika and parsley. Bring to boil. Cover and reduce heat. Simmer 1 hour, adding more water as needed. Serve in soup plates. Makes 4 servings.

# POLYNESIAN MEATBALLS

Steamed rice is a must for this fabulous dish.

| | |
|---|---|
| 1 lb. ground chuck | 1/2 cup water |
| 1 egg | 3 tbs. cornstarch |
| 1 tbs. cornstarch | 1 tbs. soy sauce |
| 1 tsp. salt | 3 tbs. vinegar |
| 2 tbs. minced onion | 6 tbs. water |
| 1/4 tsp. pepper | 1/2 cup sugar |
| 1 tbs. oil | 4 slices pineapple, chopped |
| 1 cup pineapple juice | 3 bell peppers, cut into thin strips |

Mix beef, egg, cornstarch, salt, onion and pepper. Shape into 1-inch balls. Heat large skillet and brown meatballs on all sides. Remove meatballs and drain off fat. Heat oil in skillet. Add pineapple juice and simmer 2 minutes. Mix cornstarch, soy sauce, vinegar, water and sugar. Add to pineapple juice, stirring constantly until mixture thickens. Add meatballs, pineapple and bell peppers to sauce. Heat thoroughly. Serve over rice. Makes 6 servings.

# PORCUPINES

Use lean meat for these tasty meatballs.

1 egg
1/2 cup water
1 packet (1-3/8 ozs.) onion soup mix
1-1/2 lbs. lean ground chuck
1/2 tsp. garlic powder
1/2 cup raw rice
1 can (46 ozs.) tomato juice
1 tsp. sugar
parsley

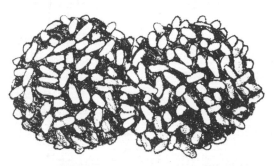

Beat egg with water and 2 tablespoons of onion soup mix. Mix with beef, garlic and 1/4 cup rice. Shape into balls. Roll balls in remaining rice, pressing lightly into meat. Heat tomato juice to boiling. Stir in remaining soup mix and sugar. Add meat balls to sauce. Cover and simmer 45 minutes or until rice puffs out of meat. Sprinkle with snipped parsley. Makes 4 to 6 servings.

# SWEDISH MEATBALLS

Serve as a main course with poppy seed noodles or as an appetizer.

1/2 lb. ground chuck
1/4 lb. ground pork
1/4 lb. ground veal
1 small onion, minced
1/2 cup dry bread crumbs
1/2 cup milk
2 eggs

1 tsp. salt
1/4 tsp. pepper
1/8 tsp. marjoram
1/4 tsp. nutmeg
1 can (10-1/2 ozs.) condensed consomme
2 tbs. flour
1/2 cup light cream

Combine meats, onion, bread crumbs, milk, eggs, salt, pepper, marjoram and nutmeg. Shape into small balls. Heat large skillet and brown meatballs on all sides. Drain off fat. Add consomme. Cover and simmer 15 minutes or until meat is thoroughly cooked. Remove meatballs. Measure broth and add enough water to make 1 cup. Sprinkle flour into skillet. Gradually add broth, stirring constantly until thickened. Reduce heat and stir in cream. Return meatballs to sauce and gently reheat. Makes 4 servings.

# SWISS MEATBALLS

1 lb. ground beef
1 lb. ground veal
1 egg, slightly beaten
1 tsp. salt
1-1/2 cups soft bread crumbs
1 tbs. chopped parsley
1 tsp. onion powder

1/2 cup milk
1 cup dry white wine
2 tbs. flour
1-1/2 cups half and half
2 cups (8 ozs.) Swiss cheese, grated
salt and pepper to taste

Combine meats, egg, salt, bread crumbs, parsley, onion powder and milk. Shape into 1-inch balls. Heat large skillet and brown meatballs on all sides. When all are cooked, drain off fat. Add wine to meatballs and simmer 10 minutes on low heat. Remove meatballs. Blend flour into pan drippings. Gradually add half and half and cheese. Stir until cheese melts. Place meatballs in sauce and heat slowly for 15 minutes. Add salt and pepper. Makes 8 servings.

# TYBO MEATBALLS

8 ozs. Tybo or Danish Blue Cheese
1 lb. ground beef
1/2 lb. ground pork
1/2 lb. ground veal
1 onion, minced
1 cup dry bread crumbs
1 cup milk
1 egg, beaten

1 tsp. salt
1/4 tsp. pepper
6 tbs. butter
4 tbs. flour
1-1/2 cups chicken broth
1 cup sour cream
1/2 tsp. **each** salt, Accent and pepper

Cut cheese in 1/2-inch cubes. Combine beef, pork, veal, onion, bread crumbs, milk, egg, salt and pepper. Mix thoroughly with wooden spoon. Pat 1/4 cup of meat mixture around each cheese cube. Shape into ovals. Melt butter and brown meatballs slowly on all sides. Remove from pan and keep warm. Stir flour into pan drippings. Cook 1 minute. Gradually add chicken broth stirring constantly. Blend in sour cream, salt, Accent and pepper. Cook over low heat until thickened. Pour over meatballs. Makes 6 to 8 servings.

# YORKSHIRE BEEF

Gorgeous to look at and divine to eat.

1-1/2 lbs. ground beef
1/2 cup cracker crumbs
1/2 cup milk
1 tsp. Jane's Krazy Mixed-Up Salt
1/4 tsp. pepper
1/4 cup melted butter
1 cup sifted flour
1/2 tsp. salt
1 tsp. Spice Islands Mixed Herbs
1/2 cup milk (room temperature)
2 eggs (room temperature), well-beaten
1/2 cup water
Mushroom Gravy, page 83

Preheat oven at 400°F. Combine beef, crumbs, milk, salt and pepper. Shape into tiny balls. Heat a large skillet and brown meatballs on all sides. Pour butter and 1/4 cup of meatball drippings into a 9 x 12-inch baking dish. Place meatballs in dish and keep warm (in 300°F. oven if you have two ovens). Combine flour, salt and mixed herbs in mixing bowl. Make a well in the center and stir in milk. Beat eggs into batter, then add water and beat until large bubbles rise to the surface. Pour batter over hot meatballs. Bake in hot 400°F. oven 20 minutes. Reduce heat to 350°F. and bake 10 or 15 minutes longer. Serve at once with Mushroom Gravy. Makes 6 servings.

MUSHROOM GRAVY

1 can (10-1/2 ozs.) cream of mushroom soup
1/2 soup can milk
1 tsp. Kitchen Bouquet
1 tbs. minced parsley

Combine ingredients. Heat, stirring occasionally. Serve in gravy boat.

# MARVELOUS MEAT LOAVES

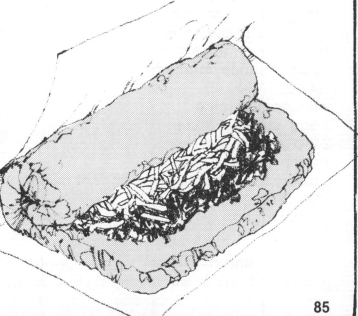

# GLAZED MEAT LOAF

1 lb. ground beef
1 lb. ground lean pork
1-1/2 cups bread crumbs
1/2 onion, minced
1 sweet pickle, minced
3/4 cup milk
2 tsp. lemon juice
1 egg, slightly beaten
2 tsp. salt
1/2 tsp. pepper
1 can (1 lb. 14 ozs.) peeled apricot halves
2 tbs. vinegar
2 tbs. catsup
1 tsp. mustard

Combine beef, pork, crumbs, onion, pickle, milk, lemon juice, egg, salt and pepper in large bowl. Mix lightly but thoroughly. Shape into loaf. Place in shallow foil-lined pan. Bake in 350°F. oven 1 hour. Drain apricot syrup into saucepan. Rub apricots through a sieve to puree. Place in saucepan with syrup. Add vinegar, catsup and mustard. Cover and simmer 15 minutes. Drain fat from meat loaf. Brush loaf with sauce. Return to oven and bake 40 minutes longer, basting with sauce several times. Remove loaf to serving platter and slice. Drain pan juices into sauce. Stir to blend. Pass sauce with meat loaf. Makes 6 to 8 servings.

# GREEK MEAT LOAF

2 pkgs. (10 ozs. ea.) frozen
    chopped spinach
1 lb. ground round
1/2 lb. ground lamb
1 onion, minced
1/2 tsp. nutmeg
1/4 tsp. cinnamon
1 cup cooked rice

3 eggs, beaten
1-1/2 tsp. salt
1/2 tsp. pepper
1 cup feta cheese, crumbled
2 tbs. lemon juice
1/4 cup catsup
3 slices bacon

Cook spinach according to package directions. Drain well and squeeze out all moisture. Combine beef, lamb, onion, nutmeg, cinnamon, rice, 2 beaten eggs, salt and pepper. Place half of mixture in 9 x 5 x 3-inch loaf pan. Mix spinach with remaining egg, feta cheese and lemon juice. Spread on top of meat layer. Cover spinach mixture with remaining meat. Brush catsup over meat and cover with bacon slices. Bake in 350°F. oven 1 hour. Place under broiler 5 minutes or until bacon is crisp. Drain off fat before slicing. Makes 6 servings.

# RAVIOLI MEAT LOAF

Accompany this satisfying entree with buttered zucchini.

1-1/2 lbs. ground chuck
1 egg
1/2 cup minced onion
1-1/2 tsp. salt
1/4 tsp. pepper
1/2 cup bread crumbs
1/4 cup milk
2 can (15-1/2 ozs. ea.) beef ravioli
1/4 cup grated Parmesan cheese

Thoroughly combine chuck, egg, onion, salt, pepper, bread crumbs and milk. Place 1/3 of meat mixture in a 9 x 5 x 3-inch loaf pan. Spread one can of ravioli on top. Sprinkle with half of cheese. Repeat layers ending with meat mixture. Pat meat firmly. Bake in 350°F. oven 1 hour and 15 minutes. Drain off fat. Allow to stand 5 minutes before slicing. Makes 6 servings.

# RUSSIAN REUBEN ROLL

1-1/2 lbs. ground beef
1 tbs. Worchestershire sauce
1-1/2 cups caraway rye bread crumbs
1 egg
1/2 cup minced onion
1/4 cup sweet pickle relish

1/4 cup thousand island or
    creamy Russian salad dressing
1-1/2 tsp. salt
1/4 tsp. pepper
1 can (16 ozs.) sauerkraut, drained
1-1/2 cups grated Swiss cheese

In a large bowl combine beef, Worchestershire sauce, bread crumbs, egg, onion, relish, salad dressing, salt and pepper. Blend ingredients well with hands. Place mixture on large sheet of waxed paper and shape into a 9 x 14-inch rectangle. Sprinkle with sauerkraut and grated cheese, leaving a one-inch border around all edges. Carefully roll the mixture, jelly-roll fashion, using waxed paper as a guide. Place in shallow baking dish and bake in 350°F. oven one hour. Makes 6 servings.

# SCANDIA MEAT LOAF

Bake one and freeze the other.

1 lb. ground beef
1/2 lb. *each* ground veal and pork
3 eggs, beaten
1 cup dry bread crumbs
2 onions, minced
2 tsp. salt
1/2 tsp. pepper
1/4 tsp. nutmeg
1/8 tsp. allspice
4 medium potatoes, boiled and mashed
3/4 cup half and half

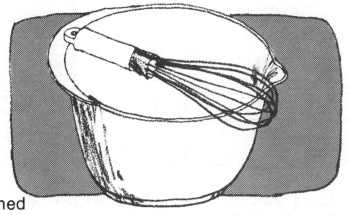

Combine all ingredients and mix thoroughly. Divide mixture and shape into 2 meat loaves. Place in shallow baking dish. Bake in 350°F. oven 45 minutes to 1 hour. Makes 8 to 10 servings.

# SICILIAN MEAT ROLL

Meat loaf never tasted so good.

2 lbs. ground beef
2 eggs, beaten
1 cup soft bread crumbs
1/2 cup tomato juice
2 tbs. parsley, chopped
1/2 tsp. oregano

1/4 tsp. salt
1/4 tsp. pepper
2 cloves garlic, minced
8 thin slices prosciutto ham
1-1/2 cups (6 ozs.) shredded mozzarella cheese
6 ozs. sliced mozzarella cheese

Combine beef, eggs, crumbs, tomato juice, parsley, oregano, salt, pepper and garlic. Place mixture on large sheet of foil and shape into a rectangle 10 x 12 inches. Arrange prosciutto slices on top of meat. Sprinkle with grated cheese. Carefully roll meat like a jelly roll, starting with short end. Place seam side down in baking dish. Bake in 350°F. oven 1 hour and 15 minutes. Place cheese slices on top of roll. Bake 5 minutes longer. Allow to stand 10 minutes before slicing. Makes 8 servings.

# SPICY MEAT LOAF

1-1/2 lbs. ground chuck
1 pkg. (1-3/8 ozs.) onion soup mix
1/3 cup rolled oats
1 egg
1/2 cup milk or dry wine
1 tsp. cumin
1 tsp. Spice Islands Beau Monde seasoning
1 tsp. Italian seasoning
1 tsp. garlic powder
2 tbs. Worchestershire sauce
1/4 cup catusp
1 slice bacon, cut in half

   Mix all ingredients except bacon. Place in loaf pan. Top with bacon. Bake in 350°F. oven 1 hour. Drain off fat. Slice and serve. Makes 6 servings.

# STUFFED MEAT LOAF

1 lb. ground chuck
1/2 lb. ground veal
1/2 lb. ground pork
1 egg
1 slice bread, crumbled
1/4 cup milk
1 tsp. salt

1/4 tsp. pepper
2 tbs. minced parsley
1 pkg. (6 ozs.) Pork Stove Top Stuffing Mix
1-1/2 cups water
3 tbs. butter
1 can (5 ozs.) water chestnuts, sliced

Combine meats, egg, bread crumbs, milk, salt, pepper and parsley. Pat half of meat mixture into bottom of 9 x 5 x 3-inch loaf pan. To prepare stuffing, combine vegetable seasoning pack with water and butter. Bring to boil. Reduce heat, cover and simmer 6 minutes. Add stuffing crumbs and stir to moisten. Remove from heat. Cover and let stand 5 minutes. Fluff with fork. Spread stuffing mixture on top of meat. Arrange water chestnuts on top of stuffing. Pat remaining meat over stuffing. Bake in 350°F. oven 1 hour and 15 minutes, or until browned. Drain off fat and allow to cool 5 minutes before serving. Makes 4 to 6 servings.

# VANCOUVER LOAF

1-1/2 lbs. ground chuck
1/2 lb. ground pork
1/2 lb. ground ham
2 cups bread crumbs
1 cup milk
1/2 cup minced onion
2 eggs, slightly beaten
salt and pepper
2 tsp. dry mustard
1/4 cup brown sugar
1/4 cup water
1/4 cup vinegar

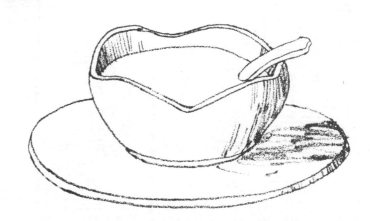

Combine meats with bread crumbs, milk, onion, eggs, salt and pepper. Shape into loaf and place in shallow baking dish. Blend mustard, brown sugar, water and vinegar. Pour sauce over loaf. Bake in 350°F. oven 1-1/2 hours. Baste occasionally. Makes 8 servings.

95

# UNUSUAL PIES AND TURNOVERS

# BURRITOS

1 lb. ground beef
3 cloves garlic, crushed
1 onion, minced
1/2 tsp. cumin
1 tsp. salt
1 tsp. chili powder
1 can (16 ozs.) refriend beans

1 can (4 ozs.) diced green chiles
2 tbs. bottled green taco sauce
12 flour tortillas
1/2 head lettuce, shredded
1 tomato, chopped
1 cup grated cheddar cheese
1 avocado, sliced

Brown beef, garlic and onion. Drain off fat. Add cumin, salt and chili powder. Cook 2 minutes. Add beans, green chiles and taco sauce. Heat, stirring until blended. Place a large spoonful of meat mixture in center of each tortilla. Top with some each of lettuce, tomato, cheese and avocado. Fold bottom up 2 inches and fold sides in to enclose filling. Place in shallow baking dish. Heat in 350°F. oven 5 to 8 minutes. Makes 12 burritos.

# CRUSTLESS PIZZA

1 lb. ground beef
2/3 cup evaporated milk
1/4 cup dry bread crumbs
2 tbs. dry onion soup mix
1/3 cup catsup
1/4 tsp. *each* basil, oregano and marjoram
1 cup sliced fresh mushrooms
1/3 cup grated cheddar cheese
1/3 cup grated mozzarella cheese
10 thin slices of dry salami
1/4 cup grated Parmesan cheese

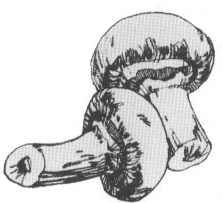

Combine beef, milk, crumbs and soup mix. Pat mixture onto bottom and sides of a 9-inch pie pan making a meat crust. Mix catsup with basil, oregano and marjoram. Spread over meat. Top with mushrooms, cheeses, salami and Parmesan. Bake in 450°F. oven 20 minutes. Cut into wedges and serve immediately. Makes 4 servings.

# CRUSTY MEAT PIE

2 tbs. sesame seed, toasted
2 cups crushed potato chips
2 egg whites, stiffly beaten
1 lb. ground beef
1 small onion, chopped
2 tbs. flour
1/4 tsp. pepper
1/2 tsp. Accent
1 tbs. chopped parsley
1 tsp. Spice Islands Beau Monde seasoning
1 can (6 ozs.) tomato paste
1 can (4 ozs.) sliced mushrooms, drained
Topping, page 101
1/2 cup crushed potato chips

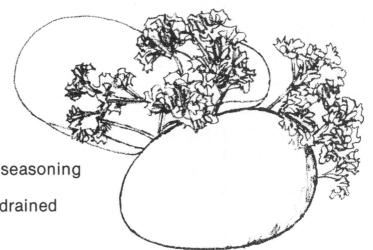

   Combine sesame seed with potato chips. Lightly fold into beaten egg whites. Pat mixture into greased 9-inch pie plate. Brown beef and onion. Drain off fat. Stir in flour, pepper, Accent, parsley and Beau Monde. Add tomato paste and mushrooms. Cook, stirring over medium heat until slightly thickened. Pour filling into crust and bake in 350°F. oven 25 minutes. Remove from oven. Spread topping over pie and sprinkle with crushed potato chips. Return to oven until cheese melts, about 5 minutes. Let stand 10 minutes before serving. Makes 4 to 6 servings.

TOPPING:

1 egg
1/2 cup milk
1/2 tsp. dry mustard
1/2 tsp. salt
1-1/2 cups (6 ozs.) grated cheddar cheese
1 tsp. Worchesterhsire sauce

Mix ingredients together well and use as directed.

# DEEP DISH BISCUIT OF BEEF

1 can (3-1/4 ozs.) French fried onions
1 lb. ground beef
1 can (4 ozs.) mushroom pieces, drained
1 can (10-1/2 ozs.) cream of mushroom soup
1 cup sour cream
salt and pepper to taste

1 can (10 ozs.) Hungry Jack biscuits
1 egg, beaten
1-1/2 tsp. Spice Islands
    Beau Monde seasoning
parsley

Reserve 1/2 cup onions for topping. Brown ground beef and drain off all fat. Transfer meat to a 3-quart casserole. Add mushrooms and French fried onions. Toss lightly. Heat soup until it comes to a boil. Remove from heat and blend in 1/2 cup sour cream, salt and pepper. Pour over meat mixture. Separate rolls and cut in half to make 20 pieces. Place rolls, cut side down, around edge and covering the center of the casserole. Sprinkle reserved French fried onions over rolls. Combine remaining sour cream, egg and Beau Monde. Pour mixture over rolls. Bake in 375°F. oven 25 minutes until rolls turn brown. Sprinkle with chopped parsley. Makes 4 servings.

# FRENCH MEAT PIE

Pastry for two-crust 9-inch pie
2 medium potatoes
1/2 cup potato liquid
1 lb. ground beef
1/2 lb. ground pork
1 small onion, chopped
1 clove garlic, minced

1 tsp. salt
1/4 tsp. pepper
1/8 tsp. cinnamon
1/8 tsp. nutmeg
1/8 tsp. powdered cloves
1 tbs. Bovril Broth and Seasoning Base
1 slice French bread

Roll out half of pastry and line pie pan. Cook potatoes. Drain and save 1/2 cup liquid. Dice potatoes. Brown beef, pork, onion and garlic. Drain off fat. Add salt, pepper, cinnamon, nutmeg, cloves, Bovril, potatoes and liquid. Tear bread into small pieces. Add to meat mixture. Simmer 10 minutes. Pour into pastry-lined pan. Top with remaining crust. Seal and flute edges. Make slits in top. Bake in 425°F. oven 20 to 25 minutes or until browned. Makes 6 servings.

# QUICHE

1 pkg. (10 ozs.) Pepperidge Farm
    Frozen Patty Shells
1 egg white
1/4 lb. bacon, diced
1 lb. ground beef

1/2 onion, chopped
1 cup whipping cream
4 egg yolks
pinch *each* salt, cayenne and nutmeg
1/2 lb. Gruyere cheese, grated

Thaw 6 patty shells. Press together well and roll out on lightly floured surface. Fit into 9 x 1-1/4-inch quiche pan. Prick bottom and sides with fork. Brush with unbeaten egg white. Saute bacon until crisp. Drain well and set aside. Brown beef with onion until meat is crumbly. Drain off all fat. Add bacon and mix well. Set aside. Blend cream, egg yolks, salt, cayenne and nutmeg. Spread meat mixture over crust. Sprinkle with cheese. Pour on custard. Bake in preheated 375°F. oven 35 minutes or until custard is set. Allow to rest 5 minutes before serving. Makes 6 to 8 servings.

# FLORENTINE PIE

This is fabulous served with sliced tomatoes.

1 lb. ground chuck
1 onion, minced
1 cup cream
1 egg yolk
3 tbs. butter
1/4 tsp. salt
1/4 tsp. nutmeg
2-1/2 cups (large bunch) finely chopped spinach
1/4 cup chopped parsley
1 cup (4 ozs.) grated Swiss cheese
4 eggs, separated
1/8 tsp. cream of tartar

    Lightly brown beef and onions until beef is crumbly. Drain off fat. Combine cream and egg yolk. Melt butter in medium saucepan. Remove from heat.

Gradually blend in egg-cream mixture. Return to heat. Stir until sauce thickens. Stir in salt and nutmeg. Add beef, onions, spinach and parsley. Simmer, un-covered, 3 minutes. Stir in cheese. Remove from heat. With spoon beat egg yolks one at a time into spinach mixture. Mixture may be refrigerated at this point and completed later. In large bowl beat egg whites with cream of tartar until stiff, but not dry. Gently fold spinach mixture into beaten whites. Turn into buttered 10-inch round casserole or baking pan with 2-inch sides. Smooth top. Bake in 350°F. oven 25 or 30 minutes or until knife inserted near center comes out clean. Cut in wedges and serve at once. Makes 6 servings.

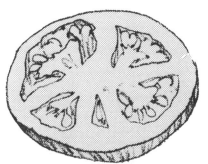
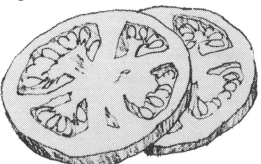

# IRISH MEAT PIE

1/2 lb. pork link sausages
2 lbs. ground chuck
1/2 cup finely crushed Hi Ho Crackers
1/2 cup milk
1-1/2 tsp. salt
1/2 tsp. pepper
1/3 cup flour
1 can (14 ozs.) beef broth
1 cup dry red wine
1 tsp. Worcestershire sauce
1 tsp. Kitchen Bouquet
1 clove garlic, crushed
1 bay leaf

1 tsp. salt
1/2 tsp. pepper
1/2 tsp. paprika
dash cloves
1 tsp. sugar
4 carrots, thickly sliced
3 tbs. flour
1/4 cup water
1 can (16 ozs.) boiling onions, drained
1 can (16 ozs.) potatoes, drained
1/2 pkg. (10 ozs.) frozen peas
1 (5-1/2 ozs.) pie crust stick

Heat skillet and brown sausages over low heat until cooked. Remove from pan and set aside. Drain fat into large saucepan. Combine beef, cracker crumbs, milk, salt and pepper. Shape into small balls. Coat with flour. Brown meatballs

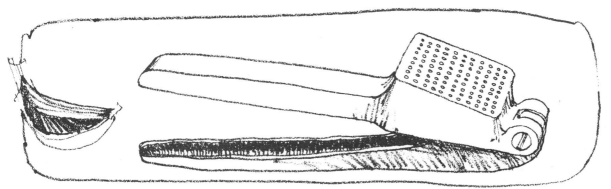

on all sides in hot sausage fat. Drain off fat. Add stock, wine, Worcestershire, Kitchen Bouquet, garlic, bay leaf, salt, pepper, paprika, cloves, sugar and carrots. Cover and simmer 20 minutes or until carrots are tender. Blend flour with water and stir into mixture. Add onions, potatoes, peas and sausages. Pour mixture into large casserole. Make pie crust as directed. Cover casserole with crust. Seal edges and slash crust to release steam. Bake in 400°F. oven about 25 minutes or until crust is brown. Makes 4 to 6 servings.

# PIROSHKI

These tasty Russian meat pies are good hot or cold. Take along to the ball game or on your next picnic.

Pastry, page 111
1 lb. ground beef
2 tbs. butter
2 potatoes, finely diced
2 cups chopped cabbage
1 onion, finely chopped
3 tbs. beef stock

2 hard-cooked eggs, chopped
2 tbs. sour cream
1 tsp. salt
1/2 tsp. pepper
1 egg
2 tbs. water

Prepare pastry as directed and chill while making filling. Saute beef until crumbly. Remove meat from pan with slotted spoon. Drain fat from pan. Melt butter in skillet and saute potatoes, cabbage and onion 10 minutes or until cabbage is wilted. Add beef stock, eggs, sour cream, salt, pepper and meat. On a floured board roll each pastry ball to a 6-inch circle. Place one 12th of mixture in center of each pastry circle. Dampen edges of the pastry with water. Fold over into half-moons and flute edges with your fingers. Make two slits in top. Lift onto baking sheet. Beat egg and water together and brush tops of pastry with mixture. Bake in the center of hot 450°F. oven 20 minutes. Reduce heat to 350°F. and bake 20 minutes longer. Allow to cool 15 minutes before serving. Makes 12 servings.

PASTRY:

4 cups flour
1-1/2 tsp. salt
1 cup lard
1/2 cup water

Sift flour and salt together. Blend in lard using pastry blender. Stir in water, adding 1 tablespoon more if necessary for a good rolling consistency. Divide pastry into 12 pieces and shape into balls. Chill.

# SPINACH PIE

Serve as an appetizer or main course along with a Greek salad for a delicious meal.

2-1/2 lbs. spinach
3 tbs. butter
1 lb. ground beef
1 small onion, chopped
1/2 cup chopped green onions
2 tbs. chopped parsley
2 tsp. dill weed

1/2 lb. feta cheese, crumbled
1/4 lb. Romano cheese, freshly grated
7 eggs, lightly beaten
1/2 tsp. nutmeg
salt and pepper to taste
1/2 lb. butter
20 sheets filo dough

Thoroughly wash spinach and remove stems. Chop and blanch in boiling water about one minute. Drain well. Melt butter in large skillet. Saute beef, spinach and onions. Drain off fat and allow mixture to cool. Stir in parsley, dill weed, feta, Romano, eggs, nutmeg, salt and pepper. Melt butter. Lay a sheet of filo dough in a buttered 9 x 13-inch baking pan. Brush with melted butter. Repeat layers of filo dough and melted butter until 10 sheets have been placed in bottom of pan. (Keep unused filo dough covered with damp towel between additions so it doesn't dry out.) Spread spinach filling evenly over filo. Cover with 10 more sheets of filo, brushing each with melted butter. Brush last sheet of filo with olive oil. Cut pie into 2-inch squares, *cutting through top layers of filo and filling only. Do not cut into bottom layer.* Bake in 350°F. oven for 1 hour or until filo is browned and pulls away from sides of pan. Cut into squares and serve. Makes 6 entree servings or 12 appetizers.

# CLASSY CASSEROLES AND ONE DISH MEALS

# ACAPULCO BEEF AND DUMPLINGS

1 lb. ground beef
2 cloves garlic, minced
1 can (16 ozs.) tomatoes
1 can (6 ozs.) tomato paste
1 onion, chopped
1/4 cup water
1 can (4 ozs.) chopped green chiles
1 tbs. chili powder
salt and pepper to taste
Dumplings, page 117

Brown meat and garlic in skillet. Drain off fat. Add tomatoes, tomato paste, onion, water, green chiles, chili powder, salt and pepper. Cover and simmer 5 minutes. Drop dumplings by rounded tablespoonfuls into hot meat mixture. Simmer, uncovered, 10 minutes. Cover and continue cooking 10 minutes longer. Makes 6 servings.

## DUMPLINGS

3/4 cup flour
1/2 cup cornmeal
2 tsp. baking powder
1 tsp. salt
1/4 cup shortening
1 cup (4 ozs.) grated sharp cheddar cheese
2 tbs. chopped cilantro or Chinese parsley
2/3 cup milk

Combine dry ingredients. Cut shortening into dry ingredients until mixture becomes coarse crumbs. Stir in cheese and cilantro. Add milk and mix until dry ingredients are moistened. Cook as directed.

# ARLENE'S STUFFED PEPPERS

1 can (8-1/2 ozs.) whole kernel corn
4 bell peppers
1/2 lb. ground beef
1/4 cup chopped onion
1 can (8 ozs.) tomato sauce
1/2 tsp. Worchestershire sauce

1/4 tsp. salt
1/4 tsp. Accent
1 cup grated cheddar cheese
1 tbs. butter
1/2 cup soft bread cubes

Drain corn and set aside. Cut green peppers in half lengthwise, remove seeds and steam in covered pan with about an inch of water for 5 minutes. Cool immediately in cold water and drain. Brown beef and onion. Drain off fat. Stir in corn, tomato sauce, Worchestershire, salt and Accent. Simmer 5 minutes. Add cheese and stir until melted. Spoon meat mixture into pepper halves. Place in baking pan. Melt butter in frying pan and saute bread cubes. Top peppers with bread cubes. Bake in 350°F. oven 20 minutes. Makes 4 to 8 servings.

# AUNTIE JO'S SPECIAL

My version of the famous New Joe's Special of San Francisco.

1 pkg. (10 ozs.) frozen chopped spinach
1-1/2 lbs. ground round
1 tbs. butter
1 onion, minced
1/4 tsp. garlic powder
1 tsp. Worchestershire sauce

1 tbs. salt
pepper to taste
5 eggs
2 tbs. heavy cream
1 cup (4 ozs.) grated cheddar cheeses

Cook spinach as directed. Drain well. Place in sieve and press to remove all water. Saute ground round just until it loses its color. Drain off fat. Add butter, onion, garlic powder, Worchestershire, salt and pepper. Saute 5 minutes. Beat eggs with cream. Add eggs and cheese to meat mixture. Scramble and serve. Makes 4 to 6 servings.

# BEEF TETRAZZINI

1-1/2 lbs. ground beef
1 onion, chopped
1 tsp. salt
1 tsp. Italian seasoning
1 can (15 ozs.) tomato sauce
1 pkg. (8 ozs.) cream cheese, softened

1 cup cottage cheese
1/4 cup sour cream
1/4 cup chopped green pepper
1/4 cup chopped green onions
8 ozs. spaghetti, cooked and drained
1/4 cup grated Parmesan

Brown beef and onion in large skillet until crumbly. Drain off fat. Add salt, Italian seasoning and tomato sauce. Beat together cream cheese, cottage cheese and sour cream. Add green pepper, green onion and spaghetti. Spread in bottom of buttered 3-quart shallow casserole. Pour meat sauce over top. Sprinkle with cheese. Bake in 325°F. oven 30 minutes. Makes 8 servings.

# CHILES RELLENOS CASSEROLE

2 cans (4 ozs. ea.) whole green chiles
1 lb. ground beef
1/2 cup chopped onion
salt and pepper
1-1/2 cups (6 ozs.) grated sharp cheddar cheese
1 cup (1/2 pint) whipping cream

1/2 cup water
4 eggs, beaten
1/2 tsp. salt
pepper to taste
several dashes Tabasco

Drain chiles. Cut in half, lengthwise. Remove seeds. Brown beef and onion. Drain off fat. Season mixture lightly with salt and pepper. Place half of chiles in 10 x 6 x 1-1/2-inch baking dish. Sprinkle with cheese. Top with meat mixture. Arrange remaining chiles over meat. Combine remaining ingredients. Beat until smooth. Pour over chiles. Bake in 350°F. oven 45 to 50 minutes or until knife inserted near center comes out clean. Sprinkle with a little grated cheese and dust with paprika, if desired. Cool 5 minutes before serving. Makes 6 servings.

# CANNELLONI

Crepes, page 167
1 lb. ground beef
1 lb. ground veal
1 small onion, minced
1/4 tsp. nutmeg
1/2 cup chopped parsley
1/8 lb. prosciutto, minced

2 eggs, beaten
3/4 cup grated Parmesan cheese
1 cup ricotta cheese
1/2 tsp. pepper
2 tsp. salt
1 can (16 ozs.) tomato sauce
Cheese Sauce, page 123

Bake crepes and set aside. Saute beef, veal and onion until meat loses color. Drain off fat. Crumble meat through fingers until very fine. Add nutmeg, parsley, proscuitto, eggs, 1/2 cup Parmesan, ricotta, pepper and salt. Mix together well. Place about 1/4 cup meat filling in center of each of 16 crepes. Roll to enclose. Pour tomato sauce in bottom of buttered 12 x 15-inch broiler-proof dish or broiler pan. Place crepes seam-side down on top of sauce. (At this point you can cover and refrigerate cannelloni overnight. Bring to room temperature before completing.) Pour Cheese Sauce over crepes and sprinkle with remaining Parmesan. Bake in 450°F. oven 10 minutes or place under broiler for 3 minutes until lightly browned on top. Makes 8 servings.

## CHEESE SAUCE

1/4 cup butter
1/4 cup flour
2 cups whole milk
1/2 tsp. salt
1/4 tsp. white pepper
1 cup grated Jack cheese
1/4 tsp. Dijon-style mustard

Melt butter in saucepan. Stir in flour. Gradually add milk. Bring to a boil and simmer 2 minutes. Remove from heat. Add salt, pepper and cheese. Stir until cheese melts. Add mustard and stir until blended.

# CHILI CON CARNE

Great for a crowd. Serve with French bread, green salad and cold beer.

1 (about 5 lbs.) chuck roast
1/4 cup oil
2 lbs. ground beef
3 onions, chopped
6 cloves garlic, minced
2 bell peppers, chopped
3 cans (1 lb. ea.) tomatoes
1 qt. water

8 tbs. chili powder
4 tbs. cocoa
1 to 2 tbs. salt
4 tsp. oregano
2 tsp. cumin
1 can (4 ozs.) diced green chiles
4 cans (1 lb. ea.) red kidney beans, undrained.

Cut meat into 1-inch cubes. Brown in hot oil. Remove cubes from pan. Brown ground beef. Drain off fat. Brown onions, garlic and bell pepper. Add beef cubes to meat mixture. Stir in tomatoes, water, chili powder, cocoa, salt, oregano, cumin and green chiles. Cover and simmer 1-1/2 hours or until meat is tender. Gently stir in kidney beans. Simmer 15 minutes. Makes 8 to 10 servings.

# EGGPLANT CASSEROLE

| | |
|---|---|
| 1-1/2 lbs. ground beef | 1 eggplant |
| 1/2 tsp. rosemary | 1 onion, thinly sliced |
| 1/2 tsp. oregano | 10 fresh mushrooms, sliced |
| 1/2 tsp. basil | 1 carton (16 ozs.) cottage cheese |
| 1 tsp. salt | 3 eggs |
| 1/2 tsp. pepper | 1/2 lb. Jack cheese, grated |

Brown meat until crumbly. Drain off fat. Add rosemary, oregano, basil, salt and pepper. Set aside. Butter and flour a large 13 x 9 x 1-3/4-inch casserole. Slice eggplant 1/4-inch thick. Quarter slices and arrange on bottom of casserole. Top with meat mixture. Place onion slices on top of meat. Add a layer of sliced mushrooms. Beat cottage cheese and eggs together. Spoon over casserole. Sprinkle grated cheese over top. Bake in 400°F. oven 1 hour. Makes 6 servings.

# ENCHILADAS

This is my mom's recipe and it's the greatest!

3 lbs. ground beef
1 clove garlic, minced
salt
3 bunches green onions
1 can (10 ozs.) Las Palmas red chili sauce
1 can (8 ozs.) tomato sauce

1 cup water
1 tsp. cumin
1 doz. corn tortillas
1 lb. sharp cheddar, grated
1 can (7 ozs.) pitted black olives

Brown meat with garlic until crumbly. Drain off fat. Add salt to taste. Finely chop onions, including green tops. Heat chili sauce and tomato sauce in saucepan. Add water and cumin. Heat tortillas until softened. Place a large spoonful of meat mixture in the middle of each tortilla. Sprinkle with onions, cheese, and drained olives. Top with a spoonful of sauce and fold both sides over. Place folded side down in large shallow baking dish. Pour remaining sauce over all. Top with any remaining onions and cheese. Bake in 300°F. oven 30 minutes. Makes 6 servings.

# FINNISH CABBAGE

4 cups shredded cabbage
1/4 cup butter
1 onion, chopped
1-1/2 cups cooked rice
1-1/2 lbs. ground round
1-1/2 tsp. salt
1/4 tsp. pepper
1/8 tsp. allspice
1/2 cup buttered bread crumbs
1/2 cup milk

Blanch cabbage in 2 quarts boiling water 5 minutes. Drain. Heat butter in large skillet. Saute cabbage and onions until tender. Set aside. Combine rice, beef, salt, pepper and allspice. Place alternate layers of meat and cabbage in buttered, 2-quart baking dish, ending with meat. Sprinkle evenly with crumbs. Using a spoon handle, punch holes to bottom of dish and pour milk over top. Bake in 350°F. oven 1 hour. Makes 6 servings.

# LASAGNE

1 lb. ground beef
1/2 lb. pork sausage
2 cloves garlic, minced
1 onion, chopped
1 can (15 ozs.) tomato sauce
1 can (16 ozs.) tomatoes
2 tbs. chopped parsley
2 tsp. sugar
2 tsp. salt
1/4 tsp. pepper
1/8 tsp. cayenne pepper
1/2 tsp. *each* marjoram, thyme,
    oregano and basil
1 bay leaf
1 pkg. (8 ozs.) lasagne noodles
2 cups cubed mozzarella cheese
2 cups (8 ozs.) grated Parmesan
1-1/2 lbs. ricotta cheese

Brown beef, sausage, garlic and onion in large saucepan. Drain off fat. Add tomato sauce, tomatoes, parsley, sugar, salt, pepper, cayenne and spices. Simmer uncovered 1 hour. Cook noodles as directed. Drain well. Pour 1/2 cup sauce into 9 x 13-inch baking pan. Alternate layers of noodles, mozzarella, Parmesan, ricotta and tomato sauce until all ingredients are used. Top layer should be sauce and grated cheese. Bake in 350°F. oven 1 hour. Makes 8 servings.

# GREEK PASTITSO

1 lb. cut macaroni
2 tbs. olive oil
2 lbs. ground beef
1 onion, chopped
1/2 cup white wine
2 tsp. salt
1/2 tsp. pepper
1/2 tsp. cinnamon
1/2 tsp. nutmeg
1 can (8 ozs.) tomato sauce
1-1/2 cups grated Parmesan cheese
2 eggs, beaten
Cream Sauce, page 131
paprika

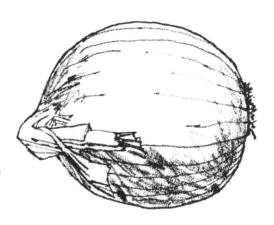

Cook macaroni. Drain and set aside. Heat oil in large saucepan. Brown beef and onions. Drain off fat. Add wine, salt, pepper, cinnamon, nutmeg and tomato sauce. Cover and simmer 10 minutes. Combine with macaroni, 1 cup cheese and eggs. Pour into greased 9 x 12-inch baking dish. Top with Cream Sauce. Sprinkle with remaining 1/2 cup cheese and paprika. Bake in 350°F. oven 30 minutes or until custard is set. Cool and cut into squares. Makes 8 servings.

CREAM SAUCE

3 tbs. butter
4 tbs. flour
1 qt. milk
4 eggs
1/2 tsp. salt
1/2 tsp. nutmeg

Melt butter in saucepan. Blend in flour. Gradually add milk, stirring constantly. Beat eggs in large bowl. Add milk mixture, a little at a time, to beaten eggs. When all is blended, add salt and nutmeg. Use as directed.

# MOUSSAKA

Serve with stuffed grape leaves and rice pilaf for a Greek party buffet.

3 (1 lb. ea.) eggplants
1/2 cup olive oil
2 tbs. salad oil
2 onions, chopped
3 lbs. ground beef
1 tbs. salt
2 cans (6 ozs. ea.) tomato paste
1-1/4 cups dry red wine

1/2 cup water
1/2 cup finely chopped parsley
1 tsp. cinnamon
1/4 tsp. nutmeg
2 cloves garlic, minced
2 tbs. flour
1 cup grated Parmesan cheese
Custard Topping, page 133

Slice eggplants in 1/4 inch slices. Pour 1/4 cup olive oil into each of 2 jelly roll or broiling pans. Dip both sides of eggplant slices into oil and arrange in pans in single layers. Bake in 425°F. oven for 15 minutes, turning occasionally. Prepare meat sauce by heating salad oil in large saucepan. Saute onions. Add ground beef. Cook, stirring until crumbly. Drain off fat. Add salt, tomato paste, wine, water, parsley, cinnamon, nutmeg and garlic. Cover and simmer 30 minutes. Remove cover and simmer until liquid is evaporated. Stir in flour and all but 1 tablespoon Parmesan cheese. Arrange half of eggplant slices in a 9 x 13-inch baking dish. Spread meat sauce over eggplant. Cover with remaining eggplant slices. Pour custard mixture over top. Sprinkle with remaining Parmesan cheese. Bake, uncovered, in 350°F. oven 1 hour. Makes 12 servings.

## CUSTARD TOPPING

| | |
|---|---|
| 1/3 cup butter | 1/8 tsp. nutmeg |
| 1/2 cup flour | 1/2 cup grated Parmesan cheese |
| 1 qt. whole milk | 6 eggs |
| 1 tsp. salt | |

Melt butter in saucepan over medium heat. Blend in flour. Cook, stirring 2 minutes. Remove from heat. Gradually add milk. Cook until thickened, stirring constantly. Add salt, nutmeg and cheese. Beat eggs slightly in large bowl. Gradually stir hot sauce into beaten eggs. Use as directed.

# MANDARIN RICE

1/2 cup rice
1 cup boiling water
1 tsp. salt
1/2 lb. ground beef
1/2 lb. ground pork
3 stalks celery, chopped
1 onion, sliced
1 cup sliced mushrooms
1 can (8 ozs.) water chestnuts, sliced

1/4 lb. fresh snow peas
*or* 1 pkg. (10 ozs.) frozen snow peas
1 can (10-1/2 ozs.) cream of
    mushroom soup
4 tbs. soy sauce
2 tbs. sherry
1/8 tsp. cayenne pepper
1/2 tsp. Accent
1 tsp. sugar

Place rice in bottom of greased 3-quart casserole. Add boiling water and salt. Set aside. Saute beef, pork, celery and onions. Drain off fat. Add mushrooms, water chestnuts and snow peas.* Combine mixture with rice. Stir in soup, soy sauce, sherry, cayenne, Accent and sugar. Cover and bake in 350°F. oven 1 hour. Makes 6 servings.

*If using frozen snow peas add 5 minutes before serving.

134

# SARMA

This recipe came from a Serbian friend and is now a family favorite.

2 lbs. ground beef
1 onion, chopped
2 cloves garlic, minced
2 tbs. raw rice
3 cans (8 ozs. ea.) tomato sauce

salt and pepper
1 head cabbage
1 tbs. vinegar
2 tbs. butter
2 tbs. flour

Brown beef, onions, and garlic. Drain off fat. Add rice, 1 can tomato sauce, salt and pepper. Boil whole cabbage in large saucepan with 2 quarts water and vinegar 10 minutes. Remove core. Separate leaves and skim off hard veins with vegetable peeler or sharp knife. To make rolls, place a spoonful of meat mixture towards small end of leaf. Fold over sides and roll towards large end. Place rolls seam side down in 9 x 13-inch baking dish. Melt butter in saucepan. Stir in flour. Gradually add remaining tomato sauce and stir until creamy. Pour over cabbage rolls. Cover and bake in 325°F. oven 1-1/2 hours. Makes 6 to 8 servings.

# SLOPPY JOE SKILLET SUPPER

A green salad and fresh fruit complete this easy meal.

1 lb. ground beef
2 cans (14 ozs. ea.) sloppy joe
1 bunch green onions, chopped
2 cans (8 ozs. ea.) tomato sauce
1 cup raw rice
1 cup (1/2 pint) sour cream

Brown beef until crumbly. Drain off fat. Add sloppy joe, onions, tomato sauce and rice. Cover and simmer 20 minutes. Blend in sour cream. Heat but do not let boil. Makes 4 to 6 servings.

136

# TAMALE CASSEROLE

Company coming? Here's a quick and delicious make-ahead casserole.

2 lbs. ground beef
1 large onion, chopped
8 (8 ozs. ea.) XLNT tamales
4 cans (8 ozs. ea.) tomato sauce
1 can (12 ozs.) whole kernal corn, drained
1 can (6 ozs.) sliced ripe olives
3 tbs. chili powder
2 cups (8 ozs.) grated cheddar cheese

Brown meat and onions. Drain off fat. Crumble tamales over bottom of large 10 x 14-inch baking dish. Add sauteed meat and onions. Combine tomato sauce, corn, olives and chili powder. Pour over tamale mixture. Top with cheese. Bake in 375°F. oven 45 minutes. Makes 8 to 10 servings.

# TERRIFIC RICE

2 pkgs. (6 ozs. ea.) mixed white
    and wild rice
1 lb. fresh sausage links
1 lb. ground beef
1/4 cup butter
1 lb. mushrooms, sliced

1/2 tsp. seasoned pepper
1 tsp. salt
1 tbs. minced onion
2 tbs. butter
1/2 lb. chicken livers
1/4 cup chopped fresh parsley

Cook rice in large saucepan according to package directions. Saute sausage in skillet 15 minutes, or until done. Add to pan with rice. Drain fat from skillet. Add beef and saute until crumbly. Drain off fat and add meat to rice. Melt 1/4 cup butter in skillet and saute mushrooms. Stir in seasoned pepper, salt and onion. Add to rice. Melt 2 tablespoons butter in skillet. Saute chicken livers until brown. Add livers to rice mixture. Toss all together and sprinkle with chopped parsley. Makes 6 to 8 servings.

# TEXAS BEEF CHILI

Our family favorite!

1 tbs. oil
1 large onion, chopped
3 cloves garlic, minced
1 bell pepper, chopped
1 lb. ground beef
2 to 3 tbs. chili powder

3 tbs. water
1 tbs. salt
1 cup raw rice
2 cans (8 ozs. ea.) tomato sauce
2 cans water

Heat oil in large saucepan. Saute onion, garlic and bell pepper. Remove from pan and set aside. Add meat to saucepan and brown, stirring to crumble. Do not allow lumps to form. Drain off fat. Add onions, garlic and bell pepper. Mix chili powder with water to form a paste. Stir into meat mixture. Add salt, rice, tomato sauce and water. Mix thoroughly. Cover and cook over low heat 1/2 hour. Remove cover and continue cooking until desired consistency. Makes 6 servings.

139

# WILD RICE CASSEROLE

This is a marvelous make-ahead party casserole.

4 cups boiling water
1 cup wild rice
1-1/2 lbs. ground beef
1 tbs. butter
1 onion, chopped
3 stalks celery, chopped
1/2 lb. fresh mushrooms, sliced
2 beef bouillon cubes
1 bay leaf
2 cans cream of chicken soup
1 tsp. garlic salt
1/2 cup slivered almonds
minced parsley for garnish

Pour 3 cups boiling water over rice. Let stand 15 minutes. Drain well. Brown beef until crumbly. Remove from pan. Drain off fat. Add butter to pan. Saute onions, celery and mushrooms. Set aside. Stir 1 cup boiling water, bouillon cubes and bay leaf together until bouillon cubes dissolve. Combine rice, beef, onions, celery, mushrooms, bouillon mixture, chicken soup, garlic salt and almonds. Place mixture in large deep casserole. Chill overnight. Bring to room temperature before baking. Bake in 350°F. oven 1 hour and 15 minutes. Garnish with snipped parsley. Makes 6 to 8 servings.

# SOMETHING DIFFERENT

# BEEF BURGERS WELLINGTON

1 pkg. Pepperidge Farms Patty Shells
1-1/2 lbs. ground round
2 eggs, slightly beaten
1 can (4 ozs.) chopped mushrooms
2 cups soft bread crumbs
1/4 cup dry red wine

2 tbs. minced onion
1 tsp. salt
1/2 tsp. crushed tarragon
1/8 tsp. lemon pepper
1 can (2-1/4 ozs.) liver pâté
Bearnaise Cream Sauce, page 145

Thaw pattie shells. Combine beef, egg, mushrooms, bread crumbs, wine, onion, salt, tarragon and lemon pepper. Mix thoroughly. Shape into 6 patties, 4-inches in diameter. Broil or pan fry 3 minutes on each side. Remove from pan and chill 1 hour. Roll out thawed patty shelves, one at a time, on a lightly floured board to make 8-inch circles. Spread liver pâté on top of each beef patty. Place a patty in the center of each pastry circle. Fold pastry over to enclose patty. Pinch edges together and place folded side down on a rimmed baking sheet. Repeat to wrap each patty. Brush pastry with beaten egg. (At this point you may cover and refrigerate overnight.) Bake in a 450°F. oven 15 minutes. Serve with Bearnaise Cream Sauce. Makes 6 servings.

144

## BEARNAISE CREAM SAUCE

2 tbs. minced shallots
1 tbs. wine vinegar
1/4 tsp. tarragon

4 tbs. butter
1/4 lb. mushrooms, sliced
1 cup whipping cream

2 egg yolks
salt and pepper to taste

In a small saucepan combine shallots, vinegar and tarragon. Boil over medium heat until liquid has evaporated. Add butter and mushrooms. Cook until mushrooms are browned. Add cream. Bring to a boil. Stir some of hot mixture into egg yolks, then return to saucepan. Cook, stirring, until slightly thickened. Serve in heated gravy boat.

GROUND BEEF WELLINGTON — Follow basic directions for Beef Burgers Wellington except shape meat mixture into 4 x 8-inch loaf. Bake in 400°F. oven 45 minutes. Chill several hours. Roll patty shells together into a rectangle large enough to cover loaf. Bake in 450°F. oven about 25 minutes or until well browned. Slice and serve immediately.

# BEEF BROCCOLI

1 tbs. oil
2 cups sliced fresh broccoli
1-1/2 lbs. ground beef
1 tsp. finely grated fresh ginger
2 tbs. soy sauce
1 onion, sliced
4 green onions, chopped

1 tsp. sugar
1/2 tsp. salt
1/4 tsp. Accent
1/4 tsp. pepper
1 tbs. cornstarch
2 cups chicken broth
1 pkg. (12 ozs.) fresh Chinese noodles

Heat oil in skillet and saute broccoli 1 minute. Remove from skillet and set aside. Combine beef with ginger and soy sauce. Add more oil to skillet if necessary. Brown sliced onions and beef until beef is crumbly. Drain off fat. Combine sugar, salt, Accent, pepper and cornstarch in medium saucepan. Gradually add chicken broth. Add broccoli, meat and green onions. Stir and cook until sauce thickens. Serve over cooked, well-drained noodles. Makes 6 servings.

# BEEF FRIED RICE

1 lb. ground beef
2 eggs
1 tbs. water
1/4 tsp. salt
1/4 cup oil
6 cups cooked rice, chilled
1 cup diced and steamed Chinese pork sausage or diced ham
1/2 cup diced green onions
2 cups chopped lettuce
1/3 cup soy sauce

Brown beef in skillet until crumbly. Drain off fat and set meat aside. Mix eggs with water and salt. Pour into skillet and cook like a crepe or pancake. Remove, cool and slice into thin strips. Separate rice. Heat oil in large skillet. Add rice and cook 5 minutes stirring constantly. Do not brown. Add egg, sausage or ham, green onions, chopped lettuce and soy sauce. Toss together and serve. Makes 6 servings.

# BEEF ROULADEN

4 strips of bacon
1 lb. ground beef
1/2 cup minced onion
3 tbs. pickle relish or chopped dill pickles

Cook bacon 2 minutes on each side. Set aside. Combine beef and onion. Flatten meat on waxed paper and shape to a 6 x 10-inch rectangle. Spread relish or pickles over meat. Lay bacon strips evenly over relish. Roll up jelly roll fashion using wax paper to help roll. Chill thoroughly. Slice into 4 slices and hold together with wooden picks. Broil 5 minutes on each side. Makes 4 servings.

# BREAKFAST SAUSAGE

1 lb. ground beef
1 lb. ground pork
2 cloves garlic, crushed
2 tsp. rubbed sage
2 tsp. salt
1/2 tsp. summer savory
1 tsp. crushed red pepper
1-1/2 tsp. marjoram
1/4 tsp. nutmeg
1/4 cup dry wine

Thoroughly mix all ingredients, using your hands to knead the spices well into the meat. Form into patties or rolls. Heat a heavy skillet. Cook sausage over low heat about 20 minutes, until well browned on both sides. Makes 8 servings.

**149**

# BENGAL BEEF

1-1/2 lbs. ground chuck
2 tbs. oil
4 onions, sliced
1 clove garlic, minced
1 tbs. curry powder
1 tbs. flour
2 tsp. salt
1/4 tsp. cardamom
1 beef bouillon cube, crumbled
1-1/2 cups water
1/4 cup vinegar
1/2 cup raisins
1/4 cup pine nuts
1/2 cup shelled pistachios
1 cup plain yogurt (optional)

    Brown beef in skillet, breaking into chunks as it cooks. Drain off fat.

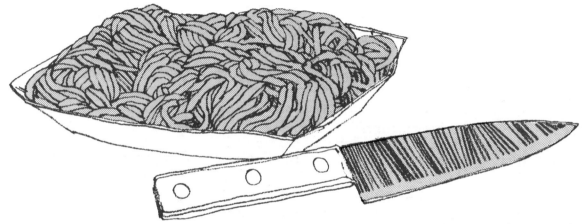

Remove meat and set aside. Heat oil in skillet. Brown onions and garlic for 20 minutes. Add curry powder and cook over low heat 2 minutes. Stir in flour and salt. Add cardamom, bouillon, water, vinegar, raisins and meat. Stir to mix well. Cover and simmer 20 minutes. Add pine nuts and pistachios just before serving. Top with yogurt if desired. Makes 6 servings.

# BEEF VALDOSTANA

Cheese Sauce, page 153
1/2 lb. ground chuck
1 lb. ground veal
4 tbs. minced parsley
4 thin slices Prosciutto ham
4 large slices of mozzarella
2 tbs. minced parsley for garnish

Prepare Cheese Sauce. Cover with plastic wrap pressed firmly against top and set aside. Combine beef, veal and 2 tablespoons parsley. Shape into 4 flat, 1/4-inch thick patties. Heat skillet and brown patties 2 minutes on each side. Remove to broiler-proof platter. Place 1 slice Prosciutto on each patty. Top each with a cheese slice. Ladle Cheese Sauce over top. Broil 5 inches from broiler for 3 to 5 minutes or until lightly golden. Sprinkle with remaining parsley. Makes 4 servings.

## CHEESE SAUCE

3 tbs. butter
3 tbs. flour
2 cups milk
1/4 cup grated Parmesan
salt and white pepper

Melt butter in saucepan and blend in flour. Gradually add milk, stirring constantly until thickened. Add cheese and stir until melted. Season with salt and pepper.

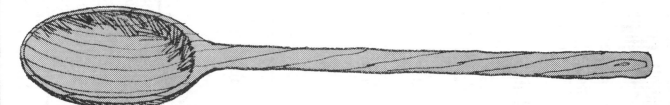

153

# CANADIAN CROQUETTES

1 lb. ground chuck
4 hard-cooked eggs, finely chopped
1 small carrot, finely chopped
1/2 onion, minced
1 tbs. sugar
1 tsp. garlic salt
1/2 tsp. ginger powder
1 tsp. Accent
1 tsp. oyster sauce or soy sauce

1 tbs. wine
1 tsp. salt
2 cups potato flakes
2 cups boiling water
1 egg, well beaten
2 tbs. water
flour
bread crumbs
oil for frying

Gently brown meat in large skillet. Drain off fat. Add chopped eggs, carrot, onion, sugar, garlic salt, ginger, Accent, oyster sauce, wine and salt. Cover and simmer 20 minutes. Measure potato flakes into large bowl. Stir in boiling water. Add meat mixture to mashed potatoes and mix thoroughly. Form into small logs 1 x 3-inches. Blend egg with water. Roll logs in flour. Dip into egg mixture and roll in bread crumbs. Deep fry in hot oil (370°F.) until brown. Drain on paper towels. Makes 4 servings.

# CUBAN PICADILLO

Serve this exotic Cuban hash with a tossed green salad or stuffed in Pita bread. It's delicious.

1 lb. ground pork
1 lb. ground beef
1 onion, chopped
1 bell pepper, chopped
1 clove garlic, minced
1 can (16 ozs.) Italian-style, peeled tomatoes
1/4 tsp. oregano
1/4 cup blanched almonds, coarsely chopped
1/4 cup seedless raisins, chopped
2 candied citrons, chopped
*or* 2 tbs. candied lemon peel

1/4 cup olives, chopped
1 tbs. capers
2 tsp. white vinegar
1 tbs. chili powder
1 tbs. chopped parsley
1 stick cinnamon
2 cloves
1/4 tsp. cumin
1 tsp. sugar
salt and pepper to taste

Brown pork and beef. Remove meat from pan. Drain off all but 1 tablespoon fat. Saute onion, bell pepper and garlic until transparent. Add tomatoes and break up with fork. Stir in oregano, almonds, raisins, citron, olives, capers, vinegar, chili powder, parsley, cinnamon, cloves, cumin, sugar, salt and pepper. Add meat and stir to mix well. Cover and simmer 30 minutes. Remove cinnamon stick before serving. Makes 6 to 8 servings.

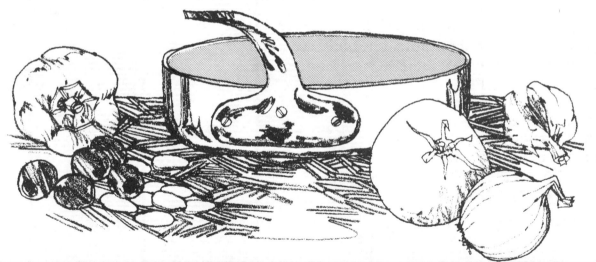

# CHINESE EGG ROLLS

1/4 lb. ground chuck
1/4 lb. ground pork
1/4 lb. raw shrimp, cleaned and shelled
1 tbs. oil
1 bunch green onions, minced
1/2 cup bamboo shoots, chopped
1 can (8 ozs.) water chestnuts, chopped
3 thin slices ginger root, minced
2 cups bean sprouts
1 tsp. Accent
2 tsp. soy sauce
2 tsp. dry sherry
1 pkg. (16 ozs.) egg roll skins
1 egg, slightly beaten
oil for deep frying

   Heat frying pan. Cook chuck and pork over high heat until meat loses all traces of pink. Chop shrimp into tiny pieces. Add to meat and cook 1 minute. Drain off fat. Remove mixture from pan and set aside. Heat oil in pan. Add green onions, bamboo shoots, water chestnuts, and ginger root. Saute or stir fry for 1-1/2 minutes. Add bean sprouts and stir fry 1 minute. Return meat-shrimp mixture to pan. Add Accent, soy sauce and sherry. Remove from heat. Transfer mixture to colander to drain and cool. Divide mixture into 16 parts. Place one part of mixture in corner of an egg roll skin. Roll skin to enclose filling, tucking in sides. Brush ends together with beaten egg. Place on a plate with seam side down. Repeat until all 16 rolls are made. Heat oil for deep frying. Fry for 4 minutes, turning to brown evenly on all sides. Drain on paper towels and serve hot. Makes 16 egg rolls.

# DOLMAS

1 jar (8 ozs.) grape vine leaves
1/2 cup raw rice
1/2 lb. ground beef or lamb
1 onion, minced
1 clove garlic, minced
1 tbs. minced parsley
2 tbs. finely chopped dill

1/4 cup pine nuts
1 tsp. salt
1/4 tsp. pepper
juice of 2 lemons
2 tbs. olive oil
1 lemon, cut in wedges
1/2 cup plain yogurt or sour cream

Drain grape leaves. Place in large bowl. Pour 1 quart boiling water over leaves. Soak 30 minutes. Carefully separate leaves. Rinse in cold water and dry on paper towels. Place 8 leaves in the bottom of a large shallow casserole. Combine rice, meat, onion, garlic, parsley, dill, pine nuts, salt and pepper. To stuff, lay grape leaves vein-side up on counter. Place about 1 tablespoon of filling on each leaf. Fold sides over filling and roll into rectangles. Do not roll too tightly because rice will expand. Pack dolmas into saucepan. Sprinkle with lemon juice and olive oil. Pour 1-1/2 cups water over top. Cover and simmer 1 hour. Garnish dolmas with lemon wedges and yogurt. Makes about 45.

# FAVORITE TOSTADAS

1/2 lb. chorizo sausage
1/2 lb. ground beef
1 can (30 ozs.) refried beans
1 tsp. salt
1 tbs. oil
8 large corn tortillas
2 cups shredded lettuce
2 tsp. wine vinegar

1 onion, finely chopped
2 tomatoes, sliced
1 can (2-1/4 ozs.) sliced ripe olives
1 large avocado, sliced
1-1/2 cups grated cheddar or Jack cheese
1/2 cup grated Parmesan
2 cups sour cream
bottled red taco sauce

Remove casing from sausage and break into small pieces. Brown sausage and ground beef together until crumbly. Drain off fat. Heat refried beans. Add salt and keep warm. Heat oil in skillet and fry tortillas until crisp. Drain on paper towels. Spread each tortilla generously with refried beans, then meat filling. Add lettuce and sprinkle with vinegar. Top with onions, tomatoes, avocado slices and drained olives. Sprinkle with cheeses and garnish with sour cream. Pass taco sauce. Makes 8 servings.

# MEREKESSH COUSCOUS

Couscous is a traditional moroccan wheat dish. It can be found where specialty foods are sold. This is delicious — I hope you will try it.

1/2 lb. ground beef
1/2 lb. ground lamb
1 onion, finely chopped
1 tsp. salt
1/4 tsp. pepper
1 tsp. ground coriander

1 tbs. butter
2 cans (10-1/2 ozs. ea.) condensed chicken broth
1 cup water
1 can (8 ozs.) garbanzos, drained
1 cup Couscous
1/2 cup chopped parsley or cilantro

Brown beef, lamb and onions. Drain off fat. Blend in salt, pepper, coriander and butter. Add chicken, broth, water and garbanzos. Cover and bring to boil. Stir in Couscous. Cover and remove from heat. Let stand 10 minutes. Just before serving stir in chopped parsley. Makes 6 servings.

# KIMA

This dish comes from the Middle East.

1 lb. ground chuck
1/4 cup butter
3 green onions
*or* 1 small onion, minced
2 tomatoes, diced
1 tbs. curry powder
1 tsp. paprika
1/2 tsp. chili powder
1/4 tsp. pepper
1/4 tsp. cayenne

2 tsp. salt
1 cup rice
2 cups chicken broth
1/2 pkg. (5 ozs.) frozen peas, thawed
condiments: shredded coconut, chutney
chopped green onions, peanuts
sliced banana
chopped hard-cooked egg
crumbled crisp bacon

Brown beef. Drain off all fat. Add butter, onions, tomatoes, curry, paprika, chili powder, pepper, cayenne and salt. Simmer, uncovered 15 minutes. Stir in rice and broth. Cover and simmer gently 30 minutes. Add peas and cook 3 minutes longer. Serve with condiments. Makes 4 servings.

# FONDUE NAPOLI

Terrific as an hors d'oeuvre or satisfying meal.

1 lb. ground beef
1 envelope (1-1/2 ozs.) Lawry's Spaghetti Sauce Mix
1 can (15 ozs.) tomato sauce
3 cups (12 ozs.) grated cheddar cheese
1 cup (4 ozs.) grated mozzarella cheese
1 tbs. cornstarch
1/2 cup dry red wine
1 loaf Italian bread, cut into bite-size pieces

Brown beef until crumbly. Drain off fat. Stir in spaghetti sauce mix and tomato sauce. Gradually add cheeses, stirring until melted. Blend cornstarch with wine and add to beef mixture. Cook and stir until thickened. Transfer and keep mixture warm in a fondue pot. Dip bread into fondue and enjoy! Makes 4 to 6 servings.

# MEAT AND MUSHROOM CREPES

Crepes, page 167
1/2 lb. ground chuck
1-1/2 cups (3/4 lb.) diced cooked ham
4 tbs. butter
1/2 lb. fresh mushrooms, sliced
2 tbs. flour
1 cup whipping cream

1/2 tsp. onion powder
1/2 tsp. lemon pepper
2 tbs. minced parsley
1 cup half-and-half
salt to taste
1 cup (4 ozs.) grated Gruyere cheese
parsley for garnish

Make crepes as directed and set aside. Gently brown beef. Drain off fat. Mix ham with beef and set aside. Heat 3 tablespoons butter in skillet. Saute mushrooms until lightly browned. Blend 1 tablespoon flour into mushrooms. Gradually add whipping cream and stir until thickened, about 8 minutes. Add onion powder, lemon pepper, parsley and meat mixture. Stir and set aside. Heat remaining 1 tablespoon butter in saucepan. Stir in remaining flour. Gradually add half-and-half. Stir over medium heat until thickened, about 7 minutes. Add salt. Place about 1/4 cup meat filling in center of each crepe. Fold both sides over and place seam side up in a buttered 9 x 13-inch baking dish. Pour cream sauce over crepes and sprinkle with grated cheese. (May be made ahead to this point and refrigerated.) Bake, uncovered, in 400°F. oven 15 minutes or until heated through and lightly browned. Makes 6 servings.

## CREPES

| | |
|---|---|
| 4 eggs | 1/2 tsp. salt |
| 2/3 cup flour | butter |
| 2 cups milk | |

Beat eggs, flour, milk and salt with rotary beater until smooth. Let stand 5 minutes. Heat 1/2 teaspoon butter in small 6-inch fry pan or crepe pan. Pour about 3 tablespoons batter in pan. Rotate pan so batter covers bottom of pan. Cook until lightly browned on bottom. Turn and lightly brown the other side. Repeat until all crepes are cooked, adding butter for each. Makes 12 to 16 crepes.

# MEXICAN LETTUCE CUPS

1 lb. chorizo
1 lb. ground chuck
2 tbs. oil
1 onion, chopped
3 cloves garlic, minced
2 tsp. chili powder
1/2 tsp. ground cumin
1 can (17 ozs.) refried beans
1 can (4 ozs.) diced green chiles
1 can (4 ozs.) sliced ripe olives, drained

2 cups (8 ozs.) grated cheddar cheese
1 tsp. salt
pepper to taste
1/2 cup sour cream
4 green onions, thinly sliced
1 avocado, peeled and diced
4 radishes, thinly sliced
1 tomato, seeded and chopped
2 large heads butter lettuce

Remove casings from chorizo and crumble into large frying pan. Add ground chuck and cook until lightly browned and separated. Remove meat and set aside. Drain off all fat. Add oil to pan and gently cook onion, garlic, chili powder and cumin until onion is limp. Stir in meat mixture, refried beans, chiles and olives. Add 1 cup cheese, salt and pepper. Place mixture in 2-quart baking dish. Sprinkle with remaining 1 cup cheese. Broil 6 inches from heat until cheese melts. Spoon sour cream in the center and garnish with green onions, avocados, radishes and tomatoes. Separate lettuce leaves. Spoon mixture into lettuce leaves, roll up and eat out of hand. Also delicious served rolled up in warmed flour tortillas. Makes 6 servings.

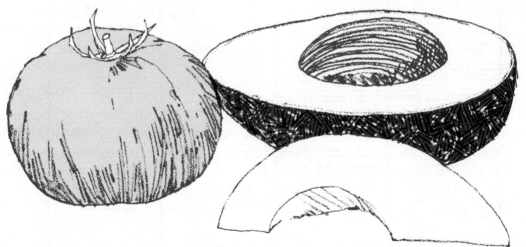

# MOROCCAN TAJINE

1 lb. ground beef
2 jars (6 ozs. ea.) marinated artichokes
1 cup raw long grain rice
1 onion, chopped
1 clove garlic, crushed
1/4 tsp. saffron
1/4 tsp. ginger
1 can (14 ozs.) chicken broth

1 tsp. salt
1/4 tsp. pepper
1/4 cup water
1/2 tsp. garlic salt
1/4 cup chopped parsley
1 can (3-1/4 ozs.) ripe olives
1 lemon, cut in wedges

Brown beef in skillet. Drain off fat. Set meat aside. Drain artichokes reserving 1/4 cup marinade. Set artichokes aside. Heat marinade in large saucepan. Add rice and cook, stirring, until lightly browned. Add onion, garlic, saffron and ginger. Cook until onion is transparent. Stir in broth, meat, salt, pepper, garlic salt and water. Bring mixture to boil, then reduce heat. Cover and simmer 20 minutes. Lightly stir in artichokes and parsley. Cover and cook over low heat until heated through. Garnish with olives and lemon wedges. Makes 4 to 6 servings.

# OYSTER BEEF AND RICE

1 lb. ground round
1 tbs. oil
4 green onions
1/2 tsp. salt
1/4 tsp. ground ginger
2 tbs. oyster sauce

pinch of sugar
1 cup hot chicken stock
1 tbs. cornstarch
1 tbs. water
4 cups hot steamed rice
1 egg (optional)

Brown beef in skillet. Drain off fat. Remove meat and set aside. Heat oil in skillet. Add onions, salt, ginger, oyster sauce, sugar and chicken stock. Cook over high heat 1 minute. Add beef to the pan. Mix cornstarch with water and blend into beef. Stir 2 to 3 minutes until thickened. Place rice on warm serving platter. Spoon beef over hot rice. Crack 1 egg and place in the center of beef and rice. Makes 4 servings.

# POTATOES GRANDE

Add your favorite seasoning or herbs to create your own variation of these stuffed potatoes.

6 large potatoes, scrubbed and oiled
1/4 cup butter, melted
1/2 cup sour cream
1 tsp. salt
1/4 cup milk
1 lb. ground beef

1 bunch green onions, minced
*or* 2 tbs. dry onion soup mix
1/2 cup chopped ripe olives
6 slices bacon, cooked and crumbled
salt and pepper to taste
1/2 cup Jack cheese

Bake potatoes in hot, 400°F. oven 1 hour. Halve lengthwise and scoop out centers, being careful not to tear shells. Place shells in shallow baking pan. Mash potatoes. Add melted butter, sour cream, salt and milk. Whip until fluffy, adding more milk if necessary. Cook ground beef in hot skillet until crumbly. Drain off fat. Add onions, olives and bacon. Fold meat mixture into mashed potatoes. Add salt and pepper. Spoon mixture into shells. Top with cheese and bake in 350°F. oven 20 minutes. Makes 6 servings.

# QUESO FONDUE

Fun and simple to prepare. Relaxed entertaining at its best!

1 lb. ground beef
1-1/2 lbs. Jack cheese, grated
1 can (10-1/2 ozs.) Aunt Penny's White Sauce
1 can (4 ozs.) diced green chiles
1 loaf French bread, cubed

Brown beef in skillet until crumbly. Drain off fat and set meat aside. Combine cheese and white sauce in ovenproof dish. Mash chiles with a fork and stir into cheese mixture. Add beef and mix well. Bake in 325°F. oven 20 minutes. Serve in chafing dish. Serve with crusty bread cubes. Also good with taco chips. Makes 4 servings.

# SPINACH CREPES WITH FONTINA SAUCE

Crepes, page 167
2 pkg. (10 ozs. ea.) frozen chopped spinach
1 lb. ground beef
1 tsp. salt
1/4 tsp. pepper
1/4 tsp. garlic powder
1/2 tsp. onion powder
1 tbs. Accent
dash nutmeg
1 can (10-1/2 ozs.) Aunt Penny's White Sauce
Fontina Sauce, page 175

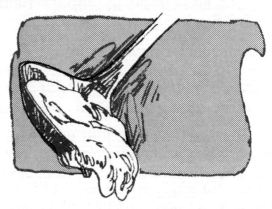

Prepare crepes and set aside. Cook spinach according to package directions. Drain well and place in wire strainer. Press to squeeze out all water. Cook beef until crumbly but not browned. Drain off fat. Break meat up between fingers until finely crumbled. Stir in spinach and remaining ingredients. Heat until thickened. Place about 1/4 cup filling in center of each of 12 crepes. Fold both sides over and place crepes seam-side down in a buttered 9 x 13-inch baking dish. Pour Fontina Sauce over crepes. Bake uncovered in 400°F. oven 15 minutes or until lightly browned. Serve immediately. (This dish may be made a day ahead and refrigerated. Bring to room temperature before baking.) Makes 6 servings.

FONTINA SAUCE

3 egg yolks
1 cup milk
2-1/2 cups grated Fontina cheese

Blend egg yolks with milk in top of double boiler. Place over simmering water. Cook, stirring constantly with wooden spoon, 7 or 8 minutes until mixture thickens enough to coat spoon. Stir in cheese and cook until cheese melts. Remove from heat immediately and let stand 10 minutes before using.

# TACO SALAD

1 cup sour cream
3 tbs. chili sauce
1 tbs. chopped green chiles
1 tbs. grated onion
1 lb. ground beef
1 onion, chopped
1 can (15 ozs.) kidney beans, drained
1 pkg. (1-1/4 ozs.) taco seasoning mix
1 tbs. chili powder

1 cup water
2 qts. salad greens
2 avocados, peeled and sliced
4 tomatoes, quartered
1 cup sliced ripe olives
2 cups slightly broken taco-
    flavored tortilla chips
1-1/2 cups (6 ozs.) grated cheddar cheese
salt and pepper to taste

Combine sour cream, chili sauce, chopped chiles and grated onion. Cover and chill to blend flavors. Brown beef and chopped onion. Drain off fat. Add kidney beans, taco seasoning, chili powder, and water. Cover and simmer 10 minutes. Drain and allow to cool. When ready to serve, thoroughly toss cooled meat mixture with lettuce, avocado, tomatoes, olives, tortilla chips, cheese and chilled sour cream dressing. Makes 8 servings.

176

# TERRY'S EGGPLANT ROMA

1 tbs. oil
1 onion, chopped
1 lb. ground chuck
salt and pepper
1 can (8 ozs.) tomato sauce
1 tbs. Italian seasoning

1 medium-size eggplant
1/4 cup olive oil
flour
1 cup grated Parmesan cheese
1 pkg. (8 ozs.) sliced mozzarella cheese
1/4 cup bread crumbs

Heat oil in large frying pan. Brown onion. Brown beef, stirring until crumbly. Drain off fat. Add salt, pepper, tomato sauce and Italian seasoning. Cover and simmer 10 minutes. Slice eggplant in 1/4-inch slices. Heat oil in large frying pan. Coat eggplant lightly with flour and brown on both sides in hot oil. Arrange half of eggplant in a 9 x 9-inch square baking dish. Spread with half of meat sauce and sprinkle with half of Parmesan. Top with half of mozzarella. Repeat layers ending with cheese. Sprinkle with bread crumbs. Bake in 450°F. oven 30 minutes until cheese and crumbs are browned. Makes 4 to 6 servings.

# VENETIAN BEEF AND ASPARAGUS

2 lbs. fresh asparagus
1 lb. ground beef
1/2 cup sour cream
2 tsp. Spice Islands Beau Monde seasoning
1/4 tsp. pepper
1/2 cup butter
2 tbs. dehydrated onion soup mix
1 tbs. minced parsley
1-1/2 cups diced mozzarella cheese
2 tbs. grated Parmesan cheese

Cook asparagus until barely tender. Drain. Brown beef until crumbly. Drain off fat. Combine beef with sour cream, Beau Monde and pepper. Set aside. Melt butter in small saucepan. Blend in soup mix and parsley. Arrange asparagus in 8-inch baking pan. Drizzle seasoned butter over asparagus. Top with meat mixture. Cover with mozzarella. Sprinkle with Parmesan. Bake 10 minutes in 350°F. oven or until cheese melts. Makes 4 servings.

# INDEX

GROUND BEEF
GROUND BEEF
GROUND BEEF
GROUND BEEF